Save Your Marriage

Improve Your Relationship While Saving Your Marriage

(Learn the Skills That Will Turn Your Personal and Couple Life Into the Success)

Kristine Barbee

Published By **Phil Dawson**

Kristine Barbee

Save Your Marriage: Improve Your Relationship While Saving Your Marriage (Learn the Skills That Will Turn Your Personal and Couple Life Into the Success)

ISBN 978-1-998927-09-8

No part of this guidebook shall be reproduced in any form without permission in writing from the publisher except in the case of brief quotations embodied in critical articles or reviews.

Legal & Disclaimer

The information contained in this book is not designed to replace or take the place of any form of medicine or professional medical advice. The information in this book has been provided for educational & entertainment purposes only.

The information contained in this book has been compiled from sources deemed reliable, and it is accurate to the best of the Author's knowledge; however, the Author cannot guarantee its accuracy and validity and cannot be held liable for any errors or omissions. Changes are periodically made to this book. You must consult your doctor or get professional medical advice before using any of the suggested remedies, techniques, or information in this book.

Table Of Contents

Chapter 1: Why Do Relationships Fail?

Do why most relationships these days are in so much trouble? From my vantage point of training, writing, and speaking approximately dating issues over the past twenty plus years, vain verbal exchange is the number one cause. After all, most of ways all and sundry interact is thru conversation. So irrespective of what the issue is, whether or not it's coins, intercourse, or children, in case you don't understand how to talk about it, you're going to have troubles.

As society has changed, so has our communication capabilities, and, I'm unhappy to say, no longer for the better. There are some of motives why this is, and why it has impacted romantic relationships in such devastating strategies. None of which I need to waste it gradual speaking approximately as it's beside the point to what I need you to understand. What subjects is which you test The Secret Language Of Long Term Lovers as rapid as possible, so you can begin to collect love, in preference to watch it die a sluggish and painful loss of lifestyles.

Another cause relationships aren't making human beings glad is because of the fact society is walking from an previous model, a model that has been exceeded down from our dad and mom and grandparents.

When human beings stayed located, they married within their village or community, or the following one over. They didn't adventure across the vicinity, or circulate sooner or later of the u . S . Like they do in recent times. Consequently, they modeled their marriage with the beneficial resource of ways clearly anybody round them did it.

Today, human beings bypass to exceptional components of the usa, float to each extraordinary u.S., or possibly marry someone they meet in their place of transport, but who moved there from somewhere some distance away. People want to mixture their backgrounds and cultural ideals approximately what a marriage need to appear like, which nobody has taught them to do.

With the Internet, topics are converting even greater swiftly. Look how the iPhone, honestly one piece of technology, has converted how humans have interaction and what is taken into consideration important. Everyone is on their cellular telephone all the time. They're expected to be available at any given 2d. They're expected to answer without delay to texts. And human beings every so often speak on the mobile phone anymore, which as a minimum permits a voice connection, with a revel in that there's a person 'real' on the alternative surrender.

The adjustments are taking place so abruptly that it's impacting the manner you have got interplay and of direction, meaning the way you speak. We don't understand what the subsequent difficulty is but a few factor's coming. You recognize that.

Modern society has changed an excessive amount of for the antique conventional version of marriage to paintings any extra. One of the largest adjustments is that we stay in a throw-away society. Unfortunately, that applies to relationships as properly.

All too rapid, at the first sign of trouble, we toss our associate apart, and very quickly, begin seeking out the following person on the way to make us experience suitable.

The irony is that in case you had the abilties to address the bumps that unavoidably display up, you will recognize a manner to use them to expose your dating into some component without a doubt lovely.

A Warning

Just studying this e-book will now not be sufficient to exchange your dating. I want it can be that easy. In order to benefit your purpose of having a rock-sturdy courting that endures, wherein love continues to broaden with each passing one year, you should make a determination to yourself, in your accomplice, and to your dating, which you need it to be the outstanding it may be, which you want to growth skills which might be going to last you for an entire lifestyles, and that you're inclined to do 'some component it takes.'

If you will make an effort to encompass those precise techniques into your each day lifestyles, your courting will alternate in dramatic and tremendous techniques.

What It Means To Settle

What I've observed through the years is that, at the same time as a pair does stay collectively, too frequently, they get into a snug region in which their dating is not what they hoped it'd be, however they don't reflect onconsideration on it very thousands as it's 'snug enough.' Tragically, what has befell is that they've 'settled.'

I've labored with sufficient human beings to recognise the lies they inform themselves. Lies like:

1.I became truly deluding myself that it'd in shape my dreams.

2.We're happier than some of the alternative couples we understand.

three.We get along nicely sufficient.

4.We're really tired from running so difficult.

5.It could be worse.

6.This is just what happens after this a whole lot time.

All those matters are actual, due to the truth that's what occurs to maximum couples that stay together. But at the same time as you compromise in and moreover you finish attempting, and also you give up to your desire for topics to be as suitable as they may be – as you'd was hoping they'll be – you're settling. I name this form of love, Platonic Love.

What Is Platonic Love

Here's an define of Platonic Love:

1.You care 'enough' approximately each distinctive.

2.You're together out of addiction and comfort.

three.You're type and considerate of every one among a kind so there's little drama.

4.You have a tendency to live separate lives with separate interests.

5.If you have got sex, it's now not very regularly, and even as you do, there's no passion.

6.You trust and appreciate every top notch.

7.You don't suppose your courting desires to be super than it's far as it's 'proper sufficient.'

Yes, there's love on this shape of dating, however you're more like buddies who love each unique, not 'lovers' who're 'in love.' In this form of marriage, you're clearly roommates. The trouble with this form of marriage is that it's lacking a lot of what's possible. I don't need that for you. Instead, I need you to experience the magic of Real Love, which, whilst you look at my description, you'll bounce up and say, "Yes, yes, I need that, too!" That's why getting to know the ones techniques is going to make this form of difference. You will now not ought to settle. Instead, you'll recognize the manner to build a relationship that is full of coronary coronary heart-melting love.

A lot of couples settle because of the reality they don't recognize some other manner. It's rare to look a pair this is loopy-in-love after years collectively. So it's commonly assumed that the everyday direction of a marriage is to settle into Platonic Love.

The number one reason there are so few couples which is probably obviously crazy in love with every different is due to the fact the competencies to make that stand up aren't taught anywhere. Even those couples which is probably glaringly in love can't certainly explain what they do in a one of a kind way than the so-called 'regular' couples.

The right information is that with what you'll research indoors the ones pages, you can apprehend the way to come to be that form of couple...and that it's much less difficult than you accept as true with you studied. You'll in no manner have to be given Platonic Love yet again.

It Doesn't Have To Be Work

Improving your relationship – maintaining it colourful, exciting, satisfied, and happy – is an ongoing way. You can't ever settle again and lighten up. Not that you could ever want to when you discover the rewards. This type of 'paintings' isn't always a burden. I communicate about putting the attempt in, which you need to art work at having a high-quality dating, however the paintings is a pleasure due to the truth you're doing it collectively, and the consequences are profound and often instant.

This is for each of you because of the truth you could enjoy your dating, and each distinct extra than you ever idea viable. When your relationship is overflowing with Real Love, your entire lifestyles will change. Everything you do, simply absolutely everyone you engage with, your paintings, your play, your own family, your pals, the entirety will beautify. So I'm excited for you...excited which you're going to be studying those new techniques...excited which you'll quickly enjoy what Real Love seems like.

My goal with this book is to encourage you to send 'the settling' on it's manner, to allow skip of being okay with 'pinnacle enough,' and to offer you the techniques required that will help you update Platonic Love with Real Love.

Can you bear in thoughts what it felt like while you didn't have a person for your lifestyles? Remember how plenty you favored to satisfy that unique man? Love is for your spirit, as air is in your lungs. It's that essential for your emotional properly-being. It's frequently stated that you have to 'paintings' to your relationship to hold it robust. I assume it looks like artwork due to the truth the 'paintings' doesn't normally start till the connection has deteriorated to the factor that immoderate measures need to be taken. Like couples treatment. That isn't always a a laugh time. And it's without a doubt paintings on the same time as honestly one in each of you is making an attempt to keep it alive, and the opposite has given up.

The art work that I am going to ask you to do is truely to exercise one easy method at a time, with the omnipresent intention of achieving Real Love, and gambling each different like in no way in advance than.

You can take a look at it like planning and searching ahead to a vacation. Because even as you start to experience this new form of love I'm speakme approximately, whilst you are living it every day, you may sense such as you're on one long, lovable excursion. That's not art work, that's play.

What's extremely good is that as you undergo every segment of improving your relationship, you get right away remarks. You'll start

11

noticing incredible subjects taking place proper away, retaining you inspired and captivated with what's taking location among you.

Care and Nurturing Of Love

How a whole lot of it gradual and electricity do you spend centered for your 'to-do' listing; all of the ones stuff you do for paintings, for the children, to keep the family on foot without difficulty, charity art work, and social sports? It takes loads of time, attention, and strength, doesn't it?

Now, what about your relationship? How lots time have you ever spent over time specializing in strategies to maintain your love alive and thriving? Most couples find that they get into that comfortable region once they have come to be a devoted couple, then truly go along with the go with the flow along, assuming the entirety can be first-rate.

What if you gave your artwork that type of lazy attention? Or your own home and children? Things may want to begin falling apart, wouldn't they? But that is exactly what takes location to maximum relationships.

What usually takes area is that you don't surely keep in thoughts what your dating desires until there's trouble. So what I'm going to help you do is observe some strategies to glaringly keep your dating in the leading facet. I requested you to undergo in thoughts while you didn't have love on your existence and what that felt like. There's a motive humans look for a person with whom to percentage their lifestyles. Right now, you do have someone…so permit's take what you have got – regardless of the fact that it's only 'pretty pinnacle' – and remodel it into a few thing exceptional.

If you don't consciously attention on maintaining your accomplice and your courting a challenge, your love, even Platonic Love, will in the end die out. You'll grow to be parting, or drifting so far apart which you turn out to be being glorified roommates who slightly be aware every distinctive. Life is clearly too brief and too valuable to have a few aspect much less than Real Love.

There's an splendid analogy that I much like the usage of because it's so revealing of what happens to humans. I've heard it stated that during case you throw a frog right into a pot of boiling water, it's going to right now jump out. But if you located a frog proper into a pot of cold water, then turn the warmth up, the frog received't note the slow and slow trade in temperature and could virtually boil to loss of life.

That's a bit like what happens to human beings. You fall in love and you observed, "Oh my God, this is the notable problem. This goes to be wonderful. We're going to be one-of-a-type from every specific couple!" Then slowly however clearly, without you noticing, you emerge as slipping deeper and deeper into the abyss of Platonic Love. You end up settling due to the fact you keep in mind you studied, "This is what occurs with all relationships."

But it doesn't should be. We all understand couples which can be although passionate about each other years and years when they've been collectively, and it's lovely. So please receive as actual with that it's miles feasible for you, as nicely. You truly want to realise how.

There's a remarkable quote via manner of Einstein: "You can't treatment a trouble through using the equal interest that created it." So I'm right here that will help you kick yourselves out of your current attention of settling for Platonic Love.

Maybe you didn't study the warmth has been developing very slowly, one diploma at a time, and now you're in a pot of boiling water, and you didn't see – or experience – it coming. With your new interest, you'll have a new mind-set. And now, armed with new competencies, you'll be able to have what you need. This 'new recognition' will open the door to Real Love.

Chapter 2: Why Does Love Die?

Let's check how your beyond relationships were given began out. You met, you observed you had loads in common, you have been coming across each one among a type's versions, the chemistry emerge as fantastic, you concept approximately each different all the time, and spent every feasible second collectively, then you definately in reality have grow to be a pair.

At first it turned into magical. You felt like you have got been a definitely suitable in shape, and also you cherished every other. You loved every particular's employer. Your buddies and your circle of relatives widespread, the whole thing turn out to be best.

Then, you hit a bump. You attempted to paintings via it, but you didn't understand how. Finally, you came to the conclusion, "We don't apprehend a manner to repair it, so I bet it's now not the connection we notion it have become." One, or every of you decide it's time to toss the whole lot away.

Because you're studying this e book, there's an great risk that you've hit this kind of 'bumps.' Or in all likelihood you're feeling an amorphous enjoy of discontent, and not brilliant why.

What's been taking place, whilst you hit those bumps, is you're definitely bumping up inside the course of your versions. If you're like maximum couples, when you first were given involved with every exquisite, you've got been interested by your versions. Yes, you cherished all of the belongings you had in commonplace. That's part of what makes us fall in love, thinking, "Wow, you're like a reflect picture of me!"

However, you had been moreover very intrigued through way of the versions, through the subjects you have got been reading about every exceptional. But then at the identical time as you have got got become an entire-fledged couple (which means that you're relationship solely, dwelling together, or married) the hassle began while those versions emerge as a trouble. But sarcastically, that's moreover whilst, in case you knew the way to address those variations, you may enhance your dating as lots as the subsequent diploma, the usage of those versions as a catalyst for deeper love.

It's those very variations that could – if you knew what to do – turn your dating into some component even better than you imagined. Every time you bump up within the path of the ones variations, it's an possibility to create deeper love and intimacy. Unfortunately, that's the time when couples are maximum in all likelihood to aspect.

The purpose versions motive so the various problems between couples is because of the fact those variations are the deliver of Unmatched Needs.

Your Core Needs

After years of studying what makes humans reply to lifestyles and each unique as they do, and in search of to make enjoy of it so I can help, I've decided the three Core Needs of anybody. They are:

1.The want to be loved and characteristic a person to offer their like to;

2.The need to be visible and widespread for who they'll be; and

3.The need to be heard and understood.

On the ground, the ones appear pretty honest. The real hassle is located even as you destroy every proper all the way all the way down to their essence.

1) Yes, certainly every body wishes to be cherished and to have someone to offer his or her like to. But what everybody desires in case you need to experience cherished varies wildly, similarly to how they offer their love. So the ones differences will purpose troubles while you don't understand a way to barter round them.

2) Yes, certainly every person desires to be seen and frequently taking place for who

they'll be. How your differences come into play with this one is that you see every special via the filters of what you've located along the way, what your tradition has taught you, similarly to from past evaluations, expectations, resentments, and disappointments. So it's tough to see someone for who they may be due to the reality those filters interfere with an independent view. And due to those same filters, accepting someone is likewise difficult.

three) And sooner or later, certain, truly all people wants to be heard and understood. But we pay interest what we need to pay interest, coloured through manner of those filters, and too regularly don't recognize the way to concentrate, or we choose not to. So with all that 'interference,' there's no manner that you're going to understand every one of a kind. Not till you learn to speak on a very new level.

In the subsequent chapters, I'm going to train you the primary conversation strategies, as a manner that will help you take away the ones filters. Not to be over-dramatic, but if you don't, you don't have any danger of making Real Love.

The Need To Be Right

Another way your variations purpose troubles is your innate preference to be right and to have subjects be the manner you want them to be. That's human nature. But actually everybody has their private thoughts and mind-set of the manner topics want to be.

When you upload egos into the combination, then the choice 'no longer to be wrong,' can often end up in reality as sturdy as needing to be proper. You can see how that by myself can motive a whole lot of friction amongst humans with one-of-a-type needs and views of what a relationship – or a few thing, for that count number range – is 'supposed' too appear like.

Some of this friction stems from one seeking to get the opportunity to 'behave properly.'

But in which does the idea of the way each distinct character need to behave come from? Of path, a few comes from societal systems of what 'right' conduct need to be. Those want to do with rules, jail tips, and spiritual teachings. Most couples generally normally tend to agree on the ones issues.

But even as your idea of 'right behavior' stems from personal beliefs and behavior drawn from experience from adolescence, numerous life opinions, and on thru every courting you've had, you could become with loads of friction. If you don't understand the way to cope with it, that friction can turn out to be a fire that destroys the whole lot.

Everyone wishes matters the way they assume they want to be. That's human nature. And absolutely everyone has desires…loads of goals. Needs to be loved, to be heard, to be right, and sure, to have things the way you need them to be. But all of us is first-rate and brings their unique ideals and expectations into each relationship. The complicated aspect is how do you're pronouncing what you want to mention, so you get your dreams met, and at the same time, permit for those versions?

You Must Become Aware

Notice this week in case you begin to nag your husband approximately some component, then ask yourself, "Is this a few element that I need truely as it's the way I discover it impossible to resist; that he's not 'behaving' in step with how I expect he have to?"

If you find out it's just you desiring topics to be a high excellent way, or he's no longer behaving in keeping with your expectations, then that's at the same time as you can begin paying attention to what's happening inside you. So pretty some methods every person reacts and responds to lifestyles is clearly habits. A dependancy is something we do with out giving it any idea, in reality doing topics day in and time out, even if it motives disharmony.

You can't see what's surely taking place until you step decrease again and emerge as conscious. If you may step decrease lower back and watch your self, you'll word what you're pronouncing, word the way you're announcing it, and also you'll likely surprise your self.

Sometimes you have a valid need, however it's the way you ask for that that creates problems. If you name for or nag, you aren't going to get the form of final effects which you want. That's why the ones coronary heart-primarily based really techniques paintings, due to the fact you may discover ways to specific your desires in a whole lot extra effective approaches.

This Is What Will Shift Everything

To get your needs met, you need to discover methods to speak on this type of manner that you no longer best get what you want, but the character you're talking to will absolutely want to provide it to you.

Your goals may be pretty masses some thing, from him leaving grimy clothes spherical, now not returning your textual content as quick as you'd like, or no longer being romantic enough. Maybe you're frustrated that he doesn't respond the way you want at the same time as you attempt to tell him what you want. Or he's constantly late, which makes you revel in disrespected, or he rarely tells you he loves you.

In the quit, the wonderful of a relationship has to do with how nicely you communicate your desires, similarly to the way you negotiate spherical your variations. That can also sound daunting, however you're speedy going to find out that it's masses easier, and plenty greater extremely good than you can recollect. When you've had been given the proper skills, you will be capable of redesign every communication you ever have along with your husband (or your spouse, if you're one of these rare guys who've decided this e-book,) from in recent times beforehand. But first, allow me percentage some thing in reality crucial with you.

Trouble Starts When You Lose Control Of Your Emotions

In my 25 years of schooling women, what I've found is the maximum not unusual motive conversations skip incorrect is due to the fact ladies lose control of their emotions; from crying to screaming, and the whole lot in among. We all do it. It's no longer a few issue toward ladies, it's clearly that women are in reality greater emotional than men, and we have have been given an prolonged listing of the way we want matters to be — which includes our man.

Have you ever 'lost it,' as they are saying? Meaning your emotions spiral out of manipulate. What takes place? You don't absolutely lose it a chunk bit, do you? No. Once you get going, it escalates.

Your feelings take maintain of you, like some alien has taken over your mouth and from time to time, you frame, when you have a tendency to stomp and throw matters. On one diploma, it feels wonderful. I understand because of the truth I've finished it on some sports. That's because of the truth you experience alive, whole of fireside and strength, letting all that stuff out that has been brewing under the floor.

But…wherein did that outburst get you? Did you're making your issue, did you get his cooperation, did he thanks for helping him understand? No, it gets you nowhere, or worse, it sends you backwards. And from time to time, it's the tipping factor and he eventually receives bored to death and leaves. And worst of all, you experience awful, wishing you may turn lower returned time.

But what in case you had an effective manner to maintain your self from 'dropping it?' Would you like it if you can check a way to no longer most effective maintain your emotions from spinning out of manage, but also cause him to offer you his entire interest with care and problem?

When you operate the approach I'm approximately to educate you, you'll experience loved whilst you've stated what you want to speak, and he'll get maintain of your phrases in a manner that he may be happy you shared with him.

The reality is, an critical part of your relationship is speaking your wants to each one-of-a-kind. Most of your conversations are clearly nice chit-chat. Conversations approximately your day, what chores want to be accomplished, and gossip approximately pals and co-employees.

Where couples get in trouble is when they're attempting to speak what they want and want from each distinct. Because you don't recognize the right conversation techniques and techniques, you get frustrated, and that's while anger and blaming enter the picture. Now you may have a few different manner.

Chapter 3: What Is 'Real' Love?

Throughout this ebook you may research pretty some strategies, each designed to help you to your course towards the sort of dating you've best dreamed about. But without the primary techniques, all of the others will fall quick of what's possible. But earlier than I percentage this primary technique with you, I need to offer you my description of Real Love.

You've determined what Platonic Love is, and you noticed that it's what takes region to the sizable majority of relationships. 'Good enough,' and 'settling' should not be an preference you're inclined to in truth take transport of. Once you notice what Real Love is, it's going to probable be the high-quality preference you'll want to make.

Real Love is:

1.You search for procedures to make each unique glad.

2.You're type to, and thoughtful of, each other.

three.You placed the needs of your companion on par together with your personal.

four.You every sense your lives are greater appropriate because of the reality you're together.

five.You sit up for seeing every particular at the same time as you've been aside.

6.You experience making love with each special, and achieve this regularly.

7.You art work together towards deepening your love and intimacy.

8.You consider and admire every different.

nine.You encourage each different to pursue favored interests.

10. Your bond continues to enhance because of the truth you maintain your dating, and every different, a top priority.

Can you bear in mind residing this way? Can you experience how enlivened your spirit will enjoy? I've been in great relationships that had been mired in Platonic Love, and one which sunk all of the manner proper right down to loathing. Now that I am blessed to stay with a person who embodies every item in this listing, I can assist you to recognize that taking factor in Real Love, each and every day, is well honestly well worth incorporating those new techniques of speaking.

I invite you and your husband to have a communique about every item on this list. Write out the list and compare how your dating is now, communicate about what you'd like, and decide what you're willing to do to make every factor you need a fact. This form of conversation is exactly what builds and deepens intimacy and therefore, Real Love. In Chapter 11 you'll find out commands on getting him to participate if he's now not the type to do this sort of issue.

Chapter 4: A New Way To Speak

1st Strategy

This first technique will become the muse upon which you can gather your 'new' courting. It is of last importance because it will straight away trade the strength of all your conversations, from the instant you start the usage of it.

Do you recognize the word, 'talk your thoughts?' The widespread definition is that it way you're pronouncing what's in your mind, instead of what you consider you studied the other man or woman wants to pay attention.

It's sincerely essential that you unique yourself, and now not cowl what you actually need to mention, like I did for most of my 29-365 days marriage. But too often human beings use that as an excuse to dump what they're wondering and feeling on the opposite character, regardless of the harm they may reason. Some human beings even brag that they're capable of be 'brutally sincere' with a person. Women often inform me, "Well, I have to be able to particular myself!" What you're gaining knowledge of right right right here is all about you expressing yourself, but in a manner that you get your dreams met by way of the usage of someone who is satisfied to advantage this...Rather than you both being disappointed after the communique.

Yes, you need to say what you want to mention, however there's a manner you can accomplish that and be heard and understood. When you say it the manner I'm going to train you, not excellent will your husband stay open to listening to you, he'll in reality want to do what you request.

So, Instead of speakme your mind, I need to expose you a way to 'Speak Your Heart.'

Imagine this scenario: Your husband has accomplished some element that has dissatisfied you. Maybe he showed up an hour late for dinner without letting .

You have numerous alternatives:

1) You can do what I used to do and maintain it to your self, pretending that the entirety is without a doubt tremendous. Not this kind of unique concept, but an awful lot of ladies do that an great way to 'keep the peace.'

2) You can get indignant and 'let loose' on him, it truly is any other way of announcing, 'lose it.' That's no longer going to preserve him open to taking note of you, that you'll studies, is a prerequisite as a manner to get your needs met.

In fact, losing it's going to do the alternative. He'll close down, flow into defensive mode, and recognition on what his subsequent reaction want to be. No listening taking place there.

Or...Three) Instead of 'speaking your thoughts,' you could 'speak your coronary heart.'

How To Speak Through Your Heart

Let me guide you thru a chunk technique to reveal you how to do it...

1.Make your self comfortable for your chair and take more than one deep breaths, a laugh with every exhalation.

2.Next, near your eyes and keep to attention to your breathing.

3.Now, don't forget what it seems like at the same time as you're the maximum in love together with your

 husband.

four.Let that feeling wash over you...breathe it in.

5.Now don't forget all the ones emotions settling into your heart.

6.While you're in this relaxed country, consider something you need to speak to him about, but you're afraid to, or had been afraid it'll purpose a huge combat on the identical time as you do.

7.But this time, recollect your heart filled with all that love for him, speakme proper away to his coronary coronary heart, saying all the ones property you've been afraid to say.

How does that sense? Do you suspect you could do it? Are you inclined to attempt? If no longer, why no longer? It surely comes right all of the manner down to how badly you want your dating to reveal into Real Love.

The above exercising would possibly appear a chunk woo-woo, however the factor is to help you 'experience' loving phrases popping out of your coronary coronary coronary heart. Once you apprehend the manner it feels, then, even these days, while you communicate to him approximately how his day have become, genuinely photo loving strength going out of your coronary heart to his.

If you workout staying centered on speaking out of your coronary coronary coronary heart, all of your verbal exchange will soften, and be whole of more love. The first time you try this, you'll see what I mean.

Do You Want To Be Right Or Be Loved?

Here's a way to inspire you to want to extend the dependancy of talking from your coronary heart, in vicinity of speakme your thoughts. When you need to have one of 'the ones' kind of talks, the kind that within the past, may not have prolonged lengthy long past as you'd hoped, ask yourself this question first:

Do you want to be RIGHT, or do you need to be LOVED? If you'll suppose lower returned, on every occasion considered one in every of you started out out a communication that ended badly, I'm pretty high-quality the hassle became that someone emerge as focused on being proper, no matter what.

When you are in the midst of desiring to be right, that will become your interest. You aren't trying to be understood, and also you aren't paying any interest to how the possibility person is receiving what you're saying. Yes, you'll likely have a have a look at that they're responding, perhaps thru shutting down or getting dissatisfied, but it is not a 'provide-and-take' kind of conversation wherein every aspects are seeking to apprehend every exclusive. Instead, what's occurring is emotions have taken over the conversation.

If you really want to be heard, to make your factor, and to have an enjoyable verbal exchange, the aim desires to shift from being right to developing love. If feelings get fired up, more love will now not be the very last consequences. It's no longer possible!

Because it's clean to get going in the heat of the instant, specifically if that's been your dependancy, here's a chunk trick that will help you transfer to speakme from your coronary coronary coronary heart. Use this acronym: BROBL, to remind yourself to talk from your coronary coronary heart. It stands for: Be Right Or Be Loved. You always get to select out among the 2.

Once you get the grasp of it, it's nearly now not viable to lose control of your feelings in case you talk from your coronary heart, because it acts like a circuit breaker. Simply reminding your self to talk from your coronary heart will motive the emotional outburst which have end up constructing up, or the hurtful terms, to actually vaporize.

If your cause is to stay collectively, to not simplest stay in love but on your relationship to comply into Real Love, then isn't this really worth a attempt, no matter how hoaky it might seem?

Speaking from your coronary coronary coronary heart is the primary a part of this approach that will help you study to say what you need to say in order so that you can get your desires met.

Chapter 5: A New Way To Listen

second Strategy

I recall talking out of your heart to be the inspiration of each exceptional dating, because of the reality on the identical time as the 'heart' is lacking from your conversation...You've were given not some thing!

But there's one extra step required so one can have coronary coronary coronary heart-based totally verbal exchange.

You've in all likelihood heard it said that to be a notable conversationalist you have to first be a first rate listener. 'Speaking out of your coronary coronary heart' is one half of why this approach works so properly. The special half of is 'listening out of your coronary coronary heart.'

Here's a simple way to pay attention to him together along with your coronary heart:

1.Imagine your coronary heart establishing to his and love flowing among you,

2.Look him within the eyes whilst he's talking,

3.Really concentrate to what he's saying,

four.Don't bear in mind what you'll say at the equal time as he's achieved,

5.Always allow right compassion to be present.

When you speak and pay attention to every different together at the side of your hearts, adorable things will take place amongst you. Most important is probably the blossoming of Real Love.

By the manner, there's a financial wreck developing where I educate you a way to inspire your husband to want to discover ways to use those strategies with you. Then you could paintings together to create a dating that sparkles with Real Love, love as a manner to undergo over time.

I said speakme out of your coronary heart have grow to be the foundation of this new dating you're going to collect, however listening out of your coronary coronary heart is an same a part of that basis. Actually, listening is even extra critical than speakme.

That's because listening is a type of gift for your partner. When you listen from your coronary coronary heart, you can mechanically be greater demanding, extra compassionate, and extra respectful, all of which is probably required for Real Love to blossom.

In crucial a part of what I'm teaching you on this ebook is to increase new behavior. You can't change your lifestyles in case you don't take particular steps to dispose of old, useless conduct, and replace them with new conduct as a way to get you what you want, which in this case, is a sparkly new dating that glows with Real Love.

So this week, to help you broaden the dependancy of speakme and listening along with your coronary heart, I invite you to turn out to be absolutely aware of all your communication, with all of us, not honestly your husband. Are you the sort of man or woman – as maximum humans are – in which you're only half of of taking note of a person, searching ahead on your opportunity to jump in and say what you have to say about irrespective of the hassle recollect is? That's no longer listening. That's just anticipating your danger to mention what you want to say.

Maybe you want to counter in conjunction with your element of the argument, or you need to function your cents, or extra approximately the challenge than they do and you need to percentage what , perhaps to impress them, or perhaps make them revel in silly. Sometimes at paintings that is going on, in which there's some of opposition.

As a part of your ongoing cause of turning into extra privy to what's taking place inner you, be aware of the way you pay hobby. When you notice which you're focused on what you want to mention, or what you want to function to the verbal exchange, then shift yourself and reputation on what they're announcing. Imagine your coronary coronary heart starting up to theirs – and this may be everybody, not simply your companion – and also you'll experience a modern-day experience of compassion getting into each conversation. It's all about developing new behavior.

The purpose I communicate masses about becoming greater aware, is because of the fact you're now not going to make changes till you become privy to what desires to alternate. If you don't understand what desires to trade, why would probable you even strive it? So the purpose of masses of what I'm sharing with you is to help you emerge as greater aware so you can see what conduct are interfering together with your goals.

If your reason is to have deeper love, greater a laugh together with your companion, to deliver passion once more into your dating, then remind yourself that the entirety you're doing goes toward achieving those desires.

Chapter 6: This Kind Of Complaining Will Kill Love

As you could consider, complaining and nagging are definitely counter to you being capable of create Real Love. It keeps you angry at each different. The one at the receiving quit of complaining remains shielding and guarded due to the fact they're moving into problem all the time. Eventually, resentment builds up, and you become at that point of Platonic Love, or worse, loathing.

There are pretty a few strategies to speak anger, resentment and dissatisfaction with out the use of any phrases. Surprisingly, they will be even more unfavorable than phrases. That's why I preferred to address this early on. So proper here are a few examples.

I notion of this one the opportunity day after I have become making the mattress. I had definitely washed the sheets in advance within the day and I modified into setting the bed lower lower back collectively and I idea, "What if I changed into disappointed that

Stephen (my companion) turned into inside the one-of-a-type room and I'm doing this by myself?"

Actually, I love to do it myself because of the fact I like everything tucked in without a doubt tight. When it entails supporting me make the mattress, he's greater of a 'allow's get this finished as speedy as feasible' shape of guy. So I idea, "Okay, what ought to I do if I become disenchanted that he come to be not supporting me?" When I snapped the pinnacle sheet to get it near the alternative aspect of the mattress, it happened to me that I should snap it clearly loud, signaling my disillusioned, and he may also study. So that could be a nonverbal way of complaining that "right right here I am, making the mattress on my own and also you're in the unique room definitely performing some issue."

Another manner is to slam doors and drawers within the direction of the house. That's a actual commonplace way of complaining to allow your partner recognize you're angry or upset with out announcing a phrase.

The kitchen is a splendid place to perform a touch severe non-verbal complaining. How approximately doing the dishes loudly when you desire all people might offer help? You can do this in your youngsters, too. You could possibly slam cabinet doors and drawers, possibly talking to your self so your companion hears. But after they ask about it, do you are saying, "Oh it's not a few element," but you're definitely hoping they hold asking so that you can ultimately say what's on your thoughts?

Maybe you cry, however whilst he asks what's wrong, you are saying, "Nothing," however you desire he'll preserve asking so you can in the long run offer in. Or possibly you skip within the unique room and cry, but you need him to come after you. Then you get even greater dissatisfied at the same time as he doesn't. Men are typically quite oblivious to these gadgets, and it can be quite scary after they don't pick out up on our suggestions. I understand how this one feels because of the reality I used to try this. I suspect most girls have at one time or another. We burst off to cry in the different room however we need him to are to be had in and pass, "Oh honey, what's wrong?"

Another non-verbal manner of letting a person recognise you're dissatisfied is to preserve up on them. This is very rude, and although it appears minor, the harm it does may be massive.

Maybe you depart in a huff and no longer using a explanation of why; you in reality stroll out the door, get for your car and force off. Maybe you roll over in bed, pull difficult at the blankets, or pound to your pillow in this form of way that it's clean and obvious which you're angry, but you don't say what's happening, even after he asks.

Maybe you sigh. Again, you're looking for to permit your accomplice understand that you're disillusioned, with out announcing a few aspect, hoping he'll be aware you're disenchanted. But then, even as he asks, "What's occurring?" you reply, "It's now not something."

These are all non-verbal but they have got the electricity to do super damage in your dating.

Pay hobby this week to any non-verbal complaining sign you could have. Maybe there are some that you don't do very frequently, but now, the following time it takes place, you'll become conscious, then you could forestall doing it, or trap yourself and keep away from doing it altogether.

These styles of non-verbal complaining are poison for your dating. They create distance. It makes your companion recognise, "Oh dear, I'm in trouble over again." They don't recognise why, so what are they going to do? They're going to shy away, and be guarded. How are you capable of growth Real Love if each of you experience such as you need to guard your self from the alternative? If you think about it, you'll see that's quite crazy.

But that's what couples do. When it's obvious some thing is inaccurate, but you're now not talking up, resentment builds on every side.

Chapter 7: A New Kind Of Sharing

third Strategy

The subsequent issue is to analyze what to mention. Your words are able to doing magical matters. You just want to realise how.

You're going to discover ways to no longer exceptional get him to want to meet your desires, however deepen intimacy on the identical time.

Do you realize what's on your heart at the same time as you need something? What I imply is, at the same time as you need something, need someone to do some factor, or need a state of affairs to exchange, have you ever ever ever decided what's riding that need, from deep inner you?

That's now not constantly clean to parent out, however even as you do, it will make all of the difference. Let me display you a simple way to decide what you really want. It's feasible that you'll be surprised with the resource of the usage of what you find out about your self.

The reason you need to analyze this is as it will assist you make a decision precisely the right terms to mention a good way to get the response you choice.

1.First, near your eyes.

2.Make your self cushty for your chair and take multiple deep breaths, enjoyable with each exhalation.

3.Now think again to the very last time you initiated a communique in that you desired a few detail, and it didn't pass as you'd was hoping, that in fact, it deteriorated into some issue quite unsightly; or it come to be one greater time you didn't communicate up.

4.Think approximately the way you felt earlier than you commenced the conversation.

5.What feelings have been you feeling? Anger, harm, frustration, fear...

6.You, because of the reality the girl who is being attentive to me now, bypass once more to the lady you were in that scenario.

7.Ask her what she definitely desired? Not what you found you favored, however an emotional need that wasn't being met.

8.Wait long enough for her to provide you an answer.

9.Now which you recognize what she truely desired, take a look at it to what she idea she wanted, and the way she approached that communique.

10. Changes the entirety, doesn't it?

Now you might be asking, how is this beneficial? Well, when you have to have this type of potentially difficult conversations – likely due to the fact you're indignant, hurt, resentful, or annoyed – in advance than you speak to him, take a bit time to connect with your heart, then, the usage of the simple approach above, you can discover what 'emotional want' is at the back of what you're feeling. That's what you're virtually requesting.

Before checking in together together with your coronary coronary heart you may think you're 'honestly' irritated. But at the equal time as you do this exercise, you may discover which you're surely feeling unloved, not noted, taken as a proper, unappreciated, or disrespected.

What's essential is that you first find out what's inside the lower back of the robust emotions you're feeling in advance than speakme to him.

Sharing Your Deeper Truth

Once you recognize what's definitely taking area, right here's the manner you begin the communique. For this example, permit's make up that he modified into on the phone with you and had to cut the call short due to the reality he had to get lower back to art work. When he hung up, you have been mad, simply mad. Maybe you have got been even a piece surprised through how strong your reaction emerge as.

So you made a decision to do this loopy exercising you honestly located. You decided a quiet location to loosen up, closed your eyes, and took some deep breaths, amusing as you exhaled. Then you asked your self, "Why did I get so irritated? I knew he needed to get again to work. Why did I react so strongly?" Next, you waited for a strategy to emerge. Finally, it came to you! You placed out what the anger became all approximately.

You remembered having the same feelings even as, as a girl, your mom ignored you, or reduce you off while you attempted to speak to her. Now you may see that your reaction grow to be out of vicinity and he absolutely added on an vintage wound from your children.

Since your cause in doing this meditation is to avoid a probably heated verbal exchange, you're now excited to percent with him what you placed about yourself.

Here's an instance of what you could say in this situation. Always recollect, on the identical time as you communicate and listen together in conjunction with your coronary coronary coronary heart, love will absolutely be constructed into each communique.

Find a time whilst he's now not doing some element. Then, with gentleness for your coronary heart, you may begin with…"Remember whilst we have been speakme on the phone this afternoon and also you needed to cut the choice brief?"

He'll respond, then you could say: "Well, I want to admit that I have been given indignant. But in vicinity of blaming you, I decided to see if I need to studies why that made me so disillusioned, and I located some component charming about myself."

At this element he want to be very interested in what you have to say, so that you keep with, "I determined out that it wasn't about you reducing the decision brief, it changed into about how my mother in no way listened to me once I have become a woman, which usually made me enjoy like she didn't care. All you probable did become motive those vintage emotions from as quickly as I modified right into a infant. Thank you for assisting me to examine why I once in a while over-react. Now I obtained't be so brief accountable you, which constantly makes me sense terrible."

Part 2 Of Sharing Your Deeper Truth

Now, this subsequent component will turn your speak right proper into a absolutely coronary heart-based totally conversation. Wait for him to reply to what you've shared with him. Let me say that yet again. Wait for him to reply!

There are a few thrilling things I determined after interviewing numerous hundred men for one in every of my books, Men Made Easy. The one which applies right right here is that guys say the motive they don't speak that hundreds is due to the reality maximum ladies speak a lot that they don't supply the fellow a hazard. And after they do, the girl both cuts him off, or makes him experience like what he said come to be wrong. Or worse, desires to dissect every phrase and every nuance of what he stated.

If you need to have greater heartfelt conversations together with your husband, right here's some thing you actually need to apprehend about him. Like most men, he wants to sound smart, like he is privy to what he's speaking approximately. More appropriately, he doesn't need to sound silly. What I placed is that men do that element wherein they move quiet with a cause to plot what they want to say. This is a massive distinction between ladies and men.

When you're in the middle of a conversation, how frequently do you forestall and plan what you're going to mention? This is foreign to most girls, really so they don't phrase guys doing this. When there's a gap in the communication, ladies fill it with more communicate. Consequently, they don't offer a man time to reply, and at the same time as he does, he receives reduce off, or worse, corrected.

I name this time men take to plot what they need to mention, their 'Moment of Silence.' Throughout a verbal exchange, he might also have numerous 'Moments of Silence'...but best whilst given the chance. When ladies get together, the chatter is constant, with interruptions, trade of difficulty be counted, and every so often a couple of conversations taking vicinity without delay. We're used to it, or even experience it. But it drives guys a chunk bit crazy.

In contrast, whilst guys maintain close out, there's loads much less speak, lots of silence, and seldom any 'sharing.' Men inform me all of the time that women whinge that they want guys to speak extra, however then those equal girls don't pay attention to what the men have to mention. You need to offer him a hazard.

So decrease returned to what you've just shared with him. After explaining what you determined out approximately your self, in case you maintain quiet, he'll sooner or later say a few difficulty. When you percentage from your coronary heart, allow yourself to be inclined, avoid blaming him…(which means that you keep it about what you're feeling), and deliver him an opportunity to reply with the aid of allowing his diverse 'Moments Of Silence,' he will very probably open his coronary coronary heart to you, by way of the usage of sharing from a extra susceptible place. This is how you have got got the ones deep conversations that sense so perfect.

When you each grow to be inclined on this manner, a few aspect sweet will arise among you. But please, make certain you don't have any expectations about how the verbal exchange need to bypass. Because if you have expectancies, you aren't able to absolutely permit the magic to appear on it's very very own.

Learning to have this type of communication will take some workout, however it's genuinely really well worth it as it will deepen your love, and manual your bond like now not some thing else. That's because of the reality any time you experience safe sufficient to be susceptible with every other, intimacy will broaden. And this sort of intimacy is what holds you collectively and keeps your love alive and thriving.

Sharing what you placed out while you searched your heart to discover why you got induced is a lovely way to construct true intimacy. Of course, bodily intimacy is important for Real Love to enlarge, but emotional intimacy is wherein Real Intimacy takes area, because you can't in reality understand someone until you analyze what's in their coronary heart. Intimacy comes from feeling regular sufficient to be inclined with every awesome. If you appearance lower lower back for your failed relationships, you'll apprehend that because the intimacy – each bodily and emotional – dwindled, so did your love. Love can best evolve into Real Love at the same time as you consciously nurture intimacy.

Never neglect that Real Love requires which you preserve the fires of intimacy burning colourful. And recall me, the fires will exit if left unattended. If you honestly do need to characteristic Real Love on your courting, it's vital that you add coronary heart to all your conversations. Yes, to all your conversations.

Intimacy is what makes your relationship with him precise in reality others. And you can not have real intimacy with out the coronary heart. But be affected person with yourself because adding coronary coronary coronary heart to all of your verbal exchange will take aware attempt for some time. Just like while you first started out using a vehicle. You needed to consciously bear in mind the whole thing you likely did. But in the end, with exercising, just like driving, talking with heart turns into a dependancy, the natural way which you and your husband communicate.

But now not like studying to pressure, in this case, you're no longer nice mastering new conduct, you're removing antique behavior that have saved Real Love out of gain…conduct which have absolutely been killing the affection you had. As your capability at the use of those techniques grows, your dating turns into more harmonious, loving, and enjoyable…for you each! From there, Real Love will blossom.

Chapter 8: A New Way To Choose Love

4th Strategy

You shift the whole lot whilst you add coronary coronary heart and compassion to what you are trying to mention. Any time you pick out to speak and pay interest via your coronary heart, you're 'selecting' to function love. When you do this, there's no room for the ones antique conversations that were driven with the aid of the use of the want to be right, worry, insecurity…or any of the feelings that keep your hearts closed down.

Once you apprehend that love is a desire every and every second of each day, you can't go once more to accepting that it's k to 'move unconscious' approximately it. You can bypass unconscious, but that too might be a preference. Once you switch out to be aware of a few element, and select out to disregard it, there's that sniggling idea in the decrease returned of your thoughts pronouncing, "Hey, I'm right here. Sorry, however you may't conceal from me."

Any relationship that enjoys Real Love is constructed at the addiction of selecting coronary coronary coronary heart-based totally communication, which means you're selecting love with each verbal exchange you've got got, whether or not or no longer it's verbal, written, or non-verbal.

Every time you decide you can upload some issue for your every day life that you're studying proper right here, you are 'deciding on love.' To me, that's one of the most stunning gives you can supply to yourself, in your husband, on your children, and to the astounding gift which you are, together together with your functionality to make the ones alternatives, and sense all of the feelings which you get to experience. You're a miracle, and that is truely really worth of love, appreciation and gratitude.

When you discover a dependancy that isn't always helping you construct Real Love, it in truth desires to be replaced with a latest addiction. But you need to come to be aware of a addiction in advance than you may pick out to update it. The motive you're unaware of a dependancy is due to the fact, properly, it's a dependancy.

In your courting, you each have many conduct of interacting with every different, but you're now not aware of them. So I want you to imagine that there's a movie digital digicam for your every motion, even on each idea. You're searching your self all the time and noticing what's happening.

Becoming extra conscious and further privy to your habits of what and how you do subjects inside the direction of the day is the first step in switching your habits round so you emerge as with the conduct of communique so you can continuously construct Real Love.

When Stephen and I first have become a pair, we marveled that it saved getting better and higher. I assumed that in the end it would degree out. But it hasn't. It's not like we're going better and better into the clouds, it's surely that our love for each extraordinary expands, turns into richer, deeper, and more satisfying. You should have that too, so long as you still chose love. Put Awareness On Hyper-Alert

Since there's not a real virtual digital camera, permit your recognition emerge as your virtual camera. Throughout the day, remind your self to be aware of what you assert, the way you say it, and what you're feeling inner. With this new interest, each time you find yourself reacting and responding to a person or situation in a manner that is counter in your motive of constructing love, ask yourself what might be causing your response. Is it about needing to be right as an opportunity of selecting to be loved? That's when it's time to remind yourself of BROBL, be proper or be loved.

It's a desire. It's all a preference. One of the matters I talk about all the time within the entire problem that I educate is which you are in a normal kingdom of preference. Even loving is a desire. How you speak collectively in conjunction with your companion is a preference to construct love or tear it apart. It's that easy.

Women regularly inform me, "I couldn't help myself" when they provide an explanation for how they stated or did a few issue that backfired on them. That isn't always genuine. If it were their boss, they'll have decided on to govern themselves. It can be the same together together together with your husband, while you're making the selection to accomplish that. I say, Choose Love!

The excellent manner you can assemble Real Love is at the same time as you each experience like winners. Part of approaches you do this is to live linked, coronary coronary heart-to-heart, and remind yourselves all of the time of every excellent's Core Needs. When you do, your coronary coronary heart stays open and compassion is omnipresent.

You'll discover that during a brief time, your new coronary heart-based totally definitely definitely verbal exchange turns into a dependancy, a herbal element you, walking within the historic beyond, like your running software program. It may be some factor that is there all the time, with out you having to don't forget it. When that turns into a dependancy for you, it will enjoy such as you've grew to turn out to be the moderate on in a room you hadn't found out come to be semi-darkish. You will each start to glow and those will word. It's a actually stunning issue.

If you remind yourselves of every different's Core Needs, compassion may be built in to all of your interactions. It will display up routinely, due to your willingness to peer every side of any situation. When you're centered on being proper, you're not inclined to study the state of affairs from their attitude. You emerge as so out of vicinity to your emotions, and what's happening for you, which you're unaware that there's someone else in the equation.

Every time you lose control of your emotions, genuinely remember that it become an vintage addiction that prompted it. All you want to do is discover what introduced on it, and why. Learning that lesson can 'nearly' make it worthwhile that it happened.

Right now you're inside the midst of actively building new conduct so there's a number of 'paying interest' required. Pay interest, step lower again, and ask, "Hmmm, what's that about?" and studies, observe, studies, study yourself, and approximately each different. As regularly as you could, have conversations wherein you percentage, "Wow, permit me allow you to apprehend what changed into occurring for me, and what brought on it." This is how deep intimacy is constructed.

During this 'addiction development section,' take into account that if you have huge disagreements, it's honestly your variations bumping up toward each unique. Now which you apprehend what's taking place, you can have a study yourselves, and then have conversations about it so your love and intimacy can increase and deepen.

Chapter 9: A New Way To Balance Your Needs

fifth Strategy

I need Real Love has come to be your reason. If the reason you ordered this e-book end up an amorphous choice to 'decorate your relationship,' I consider that now you've got a far clearer, greater robust concept of what's possible. As any 'fulfillment guru' will let you know, the extra clean, strong and unique your dreams are, the more likely you will attain them. From there, what separates the 'winners' from the 'losers' is winners take motion, they do the art work required to gain the ones dreams. They do 'some thing it takes.'

Gandhi stated, "Be the trade you need to appearance in the international." So frequently, we take a look at our partner and think, "Well they need to alternate. This is what they want to do," and we forget that we need to change ourselves in all of the strategies that we want our associate to trade. If you need your dating to be some component it's in no way been earlier than, you each need to grow to be the form of humans you've in no way been.

If you want your husband to be extra loving, extra considerate, more romantic, or extra traumatic approximately your environment – i.E. Picking up socks, dishes, grimy wet towels, all of the ones little irritations that might whittle away at a courting – you want to be an instance of what you want, simply so whilst you ask him to do the ones matters, you're stepping up and approximately the equal kinds of matters for him.

Here's how this approach works. You every have a list of need and goals. Most probably, those needs do now not suit. You could likely crave romance and togetherness, but he craves time in his storage running on his projects. You need a tidy residence and he wants home-cooked-food. For the whole lot that every wishes from the opportunity, you every need to step returned and take a look at the whole photo. You need to turn out to be aware of every different's wishes and the manner they in form together.

Imagine you are fifty ft above your house looking down on the 2 of you. You're watching the manner you have interaction and the manner you speak. You can see that each has a list of dreams, however they're relatively high-quality. You also can see that every is targeted on their listing. One is feeling neglected and not noted while the opposite is feeling disenchanted, irritated, and once in a while irritated.

From your birds-eye mind-set, you may see how high-quality their lists are. Just due to the reality they'll be a pair and love every other, does no longer advocate their desires are the same.

So now, from this new mind-set, appearance cautiously at what you need out of your husband, and what he needs from you. Are you giving him what he desires from you? If no longer, then you don't simply have a platform from which to air your court docket cases. It goes each techniques, doesn't it?

What Happened To Compassion

What's been out of region from maximum relationships is the element of compassion. It's no longer some element this is taught nowadays, at the least now not in phrases of our second-to-2nd interaction with the human beings in our lives.

One of the most big elements in The Secret Language Of Long Term Lovers is becoming consciously privy to your two hearts connecting. Simply which includes compassion, and seeing topics out of your associate's attitude, can also want to make a big distinction in how your relationship changes and improves. So don't forget how important it's far that allows you to move over to their element of the situation and ask, "Okay, how are they perceiving what's taking place proper right here?"

It's shape of like you've heard memories -— possibly you've lived it — wherein siblings receives together, perhaps for Thanksgiving or Christmas, and any individual will factor out some trouble that happened when they were children. And you find out that the way one sibling recalls it's miles absolutely one among a type from the manner every different sibling recalls it. That's due to the fact anyone come from our very own attitude and we overlook to go searching and note how certainly one of a type human beings are responding to the same situation. So this is especially essential in you being capable of enlarge the sort of relationship I'm talking approximately.

Chapter 10: A New Way To Get Answers
6th Strategy

Like the exercising I guided you through above, there's a meditation known as the Heart Searching Meditation that I propose you do. What you do is get very cushty, follow your breath, near your eyes, then flow inner and ask your self some component you want to approximately a scenario so one can apprehend it extra deeply, to try and recognize your very very own detail in what's going on, and to peer it out of your associate's attitude.

Actually, all of the meditations that I'll be asking you to do in the course of this collection are extraordinarily treasured, because even as you're surely thinking about a trouble, thinking, "What's this about…what's honestly going on right here," that doesn't permit you to get a real answer in your questioning. That's because of the truth whilst you're questioning, what's going through your mind are the rules that you've been taught, your expectancies, ideals, resentments, and all the floor stuff that gets in the way of you coming across what your coronary heart surely needs to tell you.

When you live in 'questioning mode,' you may't get proper of access to what's in reality bothering you, or what you really need. All those topics are underneath the ground of your every-day idea styles. When you pass inward, you may get entry to your deeper knowing.

Don't allow this to make you keep away from the ones sports activities sports. At the middle of any form of meditation is in reality a shape of deep rest. People pay attention meditation and expect woo-woo, or scary. It's not. It's simplest a way at the way to popularity on and be aware of what's genuinely going on on your coronary coronary heart. So whenever I ask you to do one of the meditations, please reap this because you could discover that it's full of remarkable statistics that's already sitting there in your coronary heart, in reality ready to come back again to the ground.

Note: All of the meditations are to be had as recordings at KaraOh.Com/out of place-language-of-love. You can download for your MP3 player, or pay attention on-line, and they'll be my present to you for no charge.

'Why' Holds All the Answers

When you need to 'remodel' your relationship, you must apprehend it doesn't appear in a single day. If there had been this sort of trouble as a magic wand that could make the entirety best, I may keep it hidden. That's because actual transformation takes time. Time to take a look at in which the troubles come from, then gaining knowledge of a manner to take what you've determined and layout new approaches of being...so as to in the end emerge as extremely good, love-enhancing behavior.

One of the maximum profound techniques you could boost up your transformation is to ask 'why.' Why is this element bothering me? Why do I need this? Why do I no longer want that? Why am I reacting this way? Why am I…? When you've got the answers to why you need or don't need a few issue, and apprehend why you react and respond as you do, you may then make magical choices as a way to take you lots more speedy in that you need to transport.

When you may quiet your mind and pass inner and ask your self why, it is able to be very revealing. You'll be surprised at what you could find out approximately yourself after which even as you get a technique to why, you may skip deeper and ask, "And why is that?" And then while you get to that solution, you may all over again ask, "Why is that?" Keep asking why until you understand you've lengthy beyond as deep as viable, and you'll get to what I call to the 'Heart Of the Matter.'

When you get to the personal element in which you clearly recognize, you'll apprehend, you'll comprehend in your intestine, "Yes, that's it, the last fact." There's no more why. You understand you've were given the answer you have got were given been looking for. The thriller is solved. Then, whilst you percentage on the facet of your husband, your hearts will really meld together in herbal intimacy of thoughts, spirit and coronary heart.

So constantly be asking 'why' due to the truth the more you understand yourself, the greater rapid you'll apprehend why you're reacting the way you are to whatever goes on. Then you'll be capable of quick-circuit that reaction so ultimately, you now not get prompted. You'll understand, "Oh, that's due to that issue that came about in my early life (or from my very last dating) and that's clearly me reacting out of fear, or some antique addiction." That's while you're in charge, as opposed to all the unconscious thoughts and ideals which have controlled you up till now.

Chapter 11: How To Get Him To Participate

I stated in advance that I might in all likelihood offer an cause of how you could get your guy to do this with you. So allow's do that now.

Men have a funny reaction to 'strolling on' or speakme approximately the relationship.' They clearly do experience like it's miles 'women's territory,' and that ladies are the specialists.

Like most guys, your husband probable believes his activity changed into to win you over, get you to like him, and need to be in a dating with him. Period. He then surpassed the relationship over to you so he need to pass again to focusing on being a awesome hunter, solving troubles, and being your hero.

It Isn't Absolutely Essential That He Do This

First, so that you gained't surrender, if he doesn't need to have anything to do with this shape of ethereal-fairy dating stuff, it isn't actually crucial for him to be worried for fine modifications to occur.

As I educate in Men Made Easy, he is going to most probably respond to the modifications you are making internal yourself, and in the way you have interaction with him. So it isn't hopeless. And it's possible that later, down the road, as your courting improves, he turns into greater open to at least a number of the strategies.

Of direction, it's better if he is going to take part, because of the reality strolling together will assist construct a more potent bond, and make enhancements extra speedy. Then you can have a excellent time your accomplishments together, as you watch and experience Real Love developing.

Finding Out What He Wants

First, you need to recognize what he values with reference to your relationship. It isn't always continually what you charge so you need to have a observe it from his angle so that you can higher understand him and talk more efficiently with him.

Here are some ideas that allows you to attempt, with some communicate you may use on him simply beneath this listing:

1. If you recognize what he'd want to 'restore' then use the talk underneath.

2.Ask him: "If you could enhance something approximately our relationship, what would it not no longer be?" If it's something you would like as properly, then art work with that.

3.Ask him if there's some detail from the happiest time (usually the start) collectively that fell away, and he'd need to carry all over again. Use the speak below.

4.Ask him if there's something you try this he wishes you wouldn't. If it's a few issue like nagging, or complaining, use that.

5.Ask him if there may be some thing he needs greater of from you, i.E. Time together, greater sex, home cooked meals, and so forth., then use that.

6.Ask him if he ought to wave a magic wand, how could he exchange/improve your courting. Use his solution inside the following talk.

Dialogue For When You Already Know What He Wants

Here's an instance of debate you can use if you already understand what he'd want to trade, each approximately you or your dating:

"Honey, you apprehend the manner you constantly say you want (call a few issue it is he would like extra of) well, I've positioned a manner to make that stand up.

"I got here across this e-book on Amazon and I count on what this feminine teaches without a doubt will art work.

"If you would like us to (list a selection of things so one can make your lives happier) greater, we will make it take place thru doing this collectively.

"You don't should do that plenty. I'll analyze the steps in case you don't need to, and offer an reason behind what we want to do. Or you may look at it your self. It could probably sound form of hokey, however it may be amusing. Are you willing to provide it a strive?"

Put the ones sentiments into your very own words. But be enthusiastic, playful, attractive, or regardless of the proper emotional kingdom must be to seize his interest. You apprehend him and what he's like. Work with how he already is, and allow him understand he received't want to do any 'heavy lifting,' which you'll do that.

Dialogue For When You Need To Find Out What He Wants:

First, ask one of the questions above that splendid suits what's going on among you proper now.

Once he offers you his answer, right here's what you are pronouncing:

"Okay, that's remarkable. I so recognize you telling me because of the truth I've located a manner to make that appear."

Then use the relaxation of the above communicate, placed into your private phrases.

If he says he's willing, you could then art work collectively to consist of the today's communication strategies into your ordinary lives. If he's hesitant, however as a minimum open, absolutely make him aware of the strategies. That manner, you can greater indirectly incorporate them into your dating. Once he sees how powerful they're, he'll come to be increasingly fascinated.

Here's a caution. Don't try and do too much at one time. Just select each technique in order and cognizance on that one. That manner he gained't experience overwhelmed.

Chapter 12: Why Does Resentment Kill Love?

Resentment is one of the maximum unfavorable forces in a relationship. I say that because I honestly have decided it to be one of the primary reasons why love dies.

Resentment begins offevolved offevolved to gather in a number of approaches. One way is whilst you don't communicate up, otherwise you don't communicate up in the right way about what you want and need from your each extraordinary. If you're now not speaking up, then you definately're in all likelihood to be a chunk bit upset with yourself, and frequently, that receives became in opposition to your companion. Or you start to resent the alternative person for no longer being able to virtually apprehend what it is you want, or an tremendous manner to observe your mind.

Maybe you communicate up within the incorrect way, and because of the reality you may be predisposed to argue, belittle, or call for, the alternative man or woman digs in their heels, not looking to satisfy your desires. In this form of scenario, you each enjoy inexperienced with envy.

Another cause resentment builds is which you have expectations that aren't being met. When you've got expectations approximately how your companion is meant to be and that they're falling quick of what and the way you hoped, idea, assumed they would be, you may start to enjoy resentful.

Or your relationship is falling quick of what you anticipated. In that case, the resentment is based in your companion's lack of ability to magically make your expectations come actual.

And of course, there are your versions that need to be worked around. When you don't understand the way to deal with those variations, how to talk approximately them, a manner to remedy them, the way to purpose them to so that the 2 of you're capable of decorate your relationships due to the ones versions, resentment starts offevolved to seep in.

Eventually, resentment finally finally ends up taking love's region. It in reality fills inside the area. You can't sense love for each fantastic on the equal time you're feeling green with envy – or every different horrible emotion. It virtually doesn't paintings that manner. So what I need you to recognize is that during case you've have been given any resentment the least bit, you want to address it now, otherwise you are not going so that you can assemble Real Love. The techniques you're reading will only be a band-resource protecting a wound.

Discovering Your Resentments

Here's an project you need to discover revealing. Because resentment is the gradual lack of lifestyles of love, I invite you to carry out a touch soul seeking to discover what resentments you might be protecting internal you. This is vital, due to the fact in case you are, you need to remove them when you have any danger of constructing Real Love.

Find a time while you could be quiet, alone and uninterrupted and do a Relaxation Meditation in that you ask your Inner Wise Self to join you. To try this, definitely ask for an photo that represents the hidden part of you that holds all of your cognizance. Then appearance ahead to an image to return to you – it may be something…someone, a flower, a mild, a rock…it doesn't bear in mind as it's absolutely some thing to help you attention your interest. Once the image has proven up for your mind's eye, ask it to help you discover what resentments you're putting right now to. As you're making your discoveries, write them down.

Once you've were given your listing, examine each item and decide whether or not or now not it needed to do with:

§ Your want to be right,

§ Your need for a few element to be the exactly as you need it to be,

§ Because you haven't spoken up about some thing that bothers you,

§ Or a few issue else.

Next, study every object on your list of resentments and transfer it round so that you can see it out of your accomplice's attitude. Think approximately their Core Needs. This will bring compassion into the way you see what's taking vicinity amongst you.

If you constantly examine every scenario from your associate's thoughts-set, you'll be higher able to decide if it's some aspect you want to let circulate of, or a few aspect you want to talk approximately. If it's some issue that you do want to talk about, with the techniques that observe, you'll realize the way to technique any communication.

Maybe you'll find out you simply need to be right, and that your manner isn't necessarily the best way. As you examine every item to your list, carry out a bit honest reflected image on what every is set. Then, have a communique about what you've discovered. As with any communique that well-knownshows what's below the ground, it'll deepen your intimacy.

Real Love can handiest take region whilst a couple looks like what's going on is a win-win state of affairs. That's why compassion should be built into all of your interactions. Only then can Real Love arise. When you want to be right or want topics to be your way and also you overlook about approximately that the other character has their desires to be right and to have matters to be their manner, you then absolutely're at an deadlock and also you cannot experience love.

Chapter 13: How Do Expectations Blind You?

Many expectations about love, romance, and ardour come from fantasies superior at the same time as we first start noticing the opportunity sex. Our images of ways topics may be 'a few day' come from fairy memories, movies, and novels. Many are definitely not viable to live as loads as. Cinderella and the Prince slightly knew each different, however we have been delivered about receive as real with they might stay 'luckily ever after,' with out a care inside the worldwide. Pretty ridiculous but beneath the ground, the impact were given embedded into our psyche.

The biggest problem with expectations and the fantasies that feed them, is that we enjoy a experience of unhappiness approximately the nation of our relationship, and worse, our partner.

Some of your expectancies are being met, however many are not. So a extremely good idea is to do an stock of your expectations. This has to do with what your expectancies had been in advance than you had your first courting, then the way you imagined it is probably earlier than you obtain into this courting.

What have been you hoping that being in a courting, being in love, being with this unique man or woman ought to appear to be? But don't bear in mind what's missing. Try to bear in mind your expectations previous to this relationship, and if you could keep in mind, any dating which you had been ever in, in addition to in advance than you began relationship. What had been your fantasies about love?

Once you have got your listing, undergo every item and be honest with your self as you ask whether or now not it's most effective a fable that doesn't wholesome with truth. No one in reality lives the Cinderella tale, or any of the fairy memories you grew up with. Being fed the ones memories, at the side of the movies and novels you've been exposed to, have plenty to do with how you think relationships want to be.

So see if the expectancies which you've carried internal you're in alignment with fact or now not. It's right to discover what your fantasies and expectations are because of the fact if a number of them aren't being met they're very likely inflicting unhappiness, which can bring about resentment, and feeling like you've been cheated.

Some of your expectations are suitable. It's natural and everyday to anticipate to be loved, to be reputable, to experience doing topics collectively, and to paintings together inside the direction of not unusual dreams. Those are the naked minimal. You probable produce other expectancies which can be what you have got got proper now. Write the ones down as well.

Have a communique approximately your expectancies using the Clearing Space method that I describe below. If you've been blaming him for no longer pleasurable any of your unreasonable, or even not viable expectations, express regret and tell him the way it has felt. If he is captivating a number of your expectations, like love and apprehend, allow him apprehend how a great deal you respect him. Hopefully, every of you've got were given finished this assignment and your verbal exchange will be -sided. If not, truely sharing what you've observed out approximately yourself want to assist deepen intimacy and build love.

If you need Real Love, not a myth, the ones unrealistic thoughts approximately what your relationship is 'intended' to seem like need to be launched. Performing a ritual is probably very powerful. In letting flow into of your expectations, you may need to write down down the ones you need to launch on a piece of paper, then with a easy coronary heart, burn it and allow it go into the ethers. Any type of liberating ritual will provide you with the closure you need so you can flow into on.

As lengthy as you hold close onto the fantasies, you're going to be in a rustic of disappointment, and the manner do you determined that makes your partner enjoy? When that's taking place, you're wearing the power of being upset and your companion goes to sense it, albeit no longer consciously. It's like an invisible wall among you.

Chapter 14: How To Guarantee Success

I've requested you to do some assignments, like springing up collectively collectively together with your resentments, expectations, and doing the severa guided meditations. If you're not familiar with this form of soul looking to investigate more about yourself, it is able to be uncomfortable for you. Or you might imagine it's stupid.

I'm asking you to do these types of objects because of the truth I realise from years of training, that that is a definitely powerful manner to make modifications for your life. Just studying a ebook isn't going to make the sort of improvements to your courting which you are looking for.

You need to end up privy to how you reply to conditions and people in case you're going in an effort to make the changes you choice. And I advise upgrades, no longer certainly trade for trade sake. Whether it's figuring out what you want to do to allow pass of resentment, or putting the techniques into practice, you want to turn out to be proactive. The excellent manner your dating will exchange might be due to the fact you are doing subjects in a distinct manner than you had been, and making improvements within yourself.

This e-book is ready enhancing your lifestyles through the usage of the use of setting up the door to an multiplied capability for happiness, pleasure, playfulness, love, and intimacy. So undergo in mind that if you experience which includes you want to save you. Remember why you registered for this software program application and what you have been hoping to get out of it.

Do each of the assignments with what I name, baby-like hobby, with an thoughts-set of, "Oh, what am I going to learn about myself now?" "How am I taking place the way to take that and eliminate the antique behavior and replace them with new lifestyles-improving, love-improving behavior?" And "How will our 'new' courting enjoy as soon as we've superior some of these new existence-improving behavior?" Let the satisfaction of discovery, and the opportunity of a current lovable marriage, hold you inspired and, I choice, motive you to do those assignments with enthusiasm.

The quality manner each person is a success at improving their lives is to 'do something it takes.' Yes, it's smooth to decide it's an excessive amount of artwork. If you don't want to do what I'm asking you to do, then ask yourself if you need your marriage to maintain on as it is. Because it's going to no longer exchange on it's very personal. You get to pick out.

Chapter 15: Getting To Know Each Other

The more you realise and are inclined to have a look at your associate, the nearer you becomes and at a miles quicker pace. Finding some bits of statistics to discover with will help offer you the peace of thoughts which you've positioned your for all time mate. You don't need to be same twins approximately the entirety, but some matters in commonplace gives you a proper away bond. Some areas together with desires and values are essential to be at the same web page for relationship achievement.

Know the History of Your Partner

Knowing some of the fundamentals inside the history of your companion and brazenly sharing your records will deliver each of you a basis to start exploring greater in-intensity. You can't be expected to remember everything in the starting however construct on information as time is going through manner of. A few of the topics to start with can be:

•Where they were born.

•Where they grew up.

•The length in their own family.

•Where their family is positioned.

•Education stage.

•Profession and task evaluations.

•Any beyond severe relationships/marriages.

•Any kids and wherein they'll be positioned.

A small quantity of facts to start will will assist you to provoke conversations that lead you to study even extra. It's important to have enough records to enjoy comfortable which you are growing a remarkable preference in partners.

Discuss Life Ambitions and Goals

What are your goals in life? Are you trying to stay in a big metropolis or have dreams of a small cottage close to the woods? Do you want fancy vehicles, or is an antique 4X4 pickup all you'll ever need and want? What are your ambitions with profession, homeownership, sales, retirement plans, and financial savings? You can discover the same data in cross returned. It's essential to ensure you and your companion have targets and desires that line up with every special or you'll end up a depressing individual.

Know their Core Values and Whether they Line up with Your Own

Core values are the cost you region on such things as honesty, integrity, art work ethic, compassion, and additional. It might be difficult to installation a long-time period relationship with someone that did a bit shoplifting or located lying to be no large deal if those are not your values as well. It's a recipe for immediate catastrophe. Most center values are set up earlier than the age of six, although it doesn't imply that values can't be introduced to and extended at some point of your life. It's correct to recognize in that you're starting and be aware in which matters align and in which there are capability issues.

What are their Tastes in Music, Movies, Books, Food?

Great conversations require an exquisite deliver of smooth pastimes and information what their tastes are in music, movies, books, meals, fashion, and all matters present day or modern-day. The higher you proportion the hard likes and dislikes of basics in existence, the broader the location is for powerful conversations. It's moreover excellent to recognize regions you can vary, at the least slightly. It can assist display you to a few element exquisite you may end up loving just as masses. Every character that loves Mexican meals in no way realized it until giving it a try. Sharing new critiques forces you to observe your favorites in a new mild. It can breathe new lifestyles into what had end up stagnant.

What is their Favorite Color, Animal, Car, and More?

Keep it going! You aren't finished in the reading technique in case you are going to grow to be a actual professional on your partner. You even though need to find out vital things like what's their favored color, favourite vehicle, favored animal, and whether or not or now not or now not they select out gold or silver. It's almost as if a floodgate opens and the conversations end up powerful and complete of essential statistics. It moreover offers lots of clues on what you may get for birthdays, holidays, and anniversaries. The sky is the restrict in asking the question but try to unfold out the wondering over a long period.

Are they a Deep Thinker or Impulsive with the resource of manner of Nature?

How someone communicates may have plenty to do with their baseline personality. You'll be capable of make observations as without problems as they are capable of see in that you sit down on the spectrum. More reserved, deep-wondering humans regularly appear to have fewer phrases to mention. They commonly have a tendency to vicinity quite a few emphasis on the terms used, but. It may be that they'll be introverted. It doesn't imply they'll be shy but greater planned and selective in movement.

A more impulsive individual is typically considered an extrovert. Although it can appear to be anywhere inside the map, the duties and conversations are skillful and accomplished in their specific way. You'll find out that the greater impulsive personalities not regularly run out of conversational subjects. Most are upbeat and appreciably energetic. Making those easy observations can element you inside the incredible instructions for beginning and continuing a verbal exchange.

What are Some of their Basic Habits?

Learning some in their simple conduct will assist make you an professional for your associate. Do they pass running every Monday and Wednesday morning? Is there a display they need to watch on Friday evenings? Do they choose to drink espresso out at the patio on their time off? Do they have got an worrying twitch to their eye if you depart a grimy dish in the sink after a nighttime snack? Studying and expertise the conduct of your associate will help you work extra in unison and assist create a happy domestic surroundings.

What do they want from a Relationship?

All additives of information you accumulate culminate in showing you what they're looking for and want from a courting. Ask the critical questions, assimilate the statistics, and use it to assist create a smoother transition into the relationship.

The Process Of Discovery And Learning About Your Partner

Learning approximately your accomplice ought to be a few component you look earlier each day. Most successful relationships are not based totally on a wonderful healthy. It's finding strategies to in shape collectively inside the uneven areas that make the difference. Finding strategies to broaden collectively is the ultimate goal.

Know What's in Their Suitcase

Every individual includes a suitcase of ideals and ideals that shape the normal view and perception of the area. Most are not comfortable with displaying this to humans they are no longer acquainted and cushty with, collectively with you, first of all. Begin unpacking this suitcase and taking a check the contents at your first opportunity. You need to be inclined to allow them get right of access to for your suitcase. Being open and sincere in communique is vital to growing collectively in preference to apart.

The Importance of Seeing the Complete Package

The method of unpacking this suitcase and giving every place an inspection begins offevolved at some point of the courting section. It's suitable to discover what your companion's beliefs are in each issue of lifestyles, love, and human interplay. How properly will they get together with human beings, even past their relationship with you? Are they capable of preserve a consistent challenge and relate nicely to friends? Are they regularly bumping heads with authority figures? Do they seem mature at the same time as it's required? It's critical to test those facts to recognize the big picture absolutely. The manner they communicate or fail to talk with others may be a caution sign that topics can damage down.

Are You Seeing Stable Moods and a Compatible Personality?

Sudden and drastic temper swings in a partner may want to make life miserable. Do they appear to have a stable countenance maximum of the time? Women can get thrown off with the aid of the usage of month-to-month hormonal modifications, but it can additionally propose their capability to address strain and tension. Talking approximately feasible stressors and methods to reduce anxiety allow you to and your associate. As long as your primary personalities look like minded, the rest is potential. Your accomplice is probably in awe that you are willing to assist them communicate via their problems and anxieties.

What Makes Your Partner Emotional?

All humans have a one-of-a-kind threshold of emotional response to the whole lot in lifestyles. Emotional control and the capacity to expose emotion are equally vital in being capable of supply emotions well. Do they've issues discussing emotional subjects? Do you need to be the best to initiate affection? It's critical to find out a glad medium that allows every of you to experience snug sharing and demonstrating emotional responses. It may be that your accomplice desires to undertaking out in their comfort quarter and experience a new way of responding to topics.

What are their Pet Peeves?

Pet peeves are little subjects that pressure humans bonkers! It's accessible to recognize what this stuff are along side your associate. You must additionally relay any of your pet peeves to them. It may want to something as slight as not loading the dishwasher the manner they commonly do the undertaking. Learning what the puppy peeves are for every of you and warding off them will help supply a more harmonious atmosphere to the house. Instead of viewing them as a piece of trivial information, take into account the way you sense on the same time as your doggy peeve is proper in the the front of you. Shoes left in the center of the ground, laundry piled in a nook in location of the abate, or some factor virtually makes your blood boil.

What are their World Views?

How does your accomplice view the location? Are there any strong political evaluations that might warfare at the aspect of your private? Are fears of a tanking global monetary device one of the first matters they communicate about every morning? The ultimate aspect anybody desires first element inside the morning is to concentrate political ranting and raving. It's nicely sincerely worth exploring what their global perspectives are and the manner you may help restrict any conflict by way of using fending off particular subjects of discussion. It's no longer the prevent of the vicinity to keep differing views.

Why Do they Hold their Particular Views?

If your partner holds robust worldwide perspectives and appears majorly opinionated, try to find out why they feel the manner they do. It's regularly a generational idea exceeded down thru families. Are they excellent sufficient together with your views being a chunk specific or a lot much less sturdy? The final aspect you need is to revel in you need to convert to any beliefs and views you are not snug with, any more than they may need to transform to yours. Most people usually generally generally tend to fall someplace in the mild variety of political and global perspectives. It's not often a massive trouble in most relationships.

Is There Any Extra Baggage?

People tend to hold greater baggage with them you may't continuously stumble on right away. It may be vintage hurts carried over from a disastrous dating or marriage. It is probably from suffering abuse as a toddler. Incidences like this that leave pain and trauma may have an impact on how they reply and deal with people. It can result in problems with accept as true with or fears of abandonment. You want to pay interest for some key phrases at the identical time as all of those numerous subjects are mentioned. Some terms to search for are:

•Divorce – parental or their very own.

- Child custody problems.

- Child abuse.

- Spousal or partner abuse.

- Alcoholic or drug addict upbringing.

- Cheating associate.

How to Become an Expert Baggage Handler

The truth that a person is wearing a touch greater luggage doesn't cause them to a terrible capability companion. It might also additionally take time and staying power to win over their trust definitely. Your accomplice may likely mechanically begin to enjoy excessive degrees of hysteria in case you don't make it domestic right when predicted and rush to anticipate you're dishonest. Keep your cell telephone accessible and phone in case you are walking past due. A little gesture like this could help positioned their mind comfy and maintain them out of an older, awful region.

Chapter 16: Drawing A Path Together: Your Expectations, Mutual Trust, Your Strengths, And Your Commitment As A Couple

Identifying Your Strengths and Problem Areas

The element of touch without problems disappears from view in warfare conditions. Situations emerge as exaggerated while simply all people tries to steer or weaken. It isn't sudden that people overlook about about areas of mutual interest, lose the capability to apprehend, study and rely upon what they have already got in not unusual.

Create a common interest in marriage

By accepting a person you disagree with, you can revel in which you are dropping floor. But a have a study positioned that powerful negotiators flip to regions of settlement 3 times extra regularly than inactive negotiators. The element of touch is critical for resolving a battle due to the fact it's miles frequently forgotten or uncared for. If no person is looking for a common language, how will or no longer it is built?

Remember the conflict scenario for your life even as you and the opposite character favored to apprehend it, however it were given worse. Are you thinking about in which the not unusual detail become amongst you?

Types of common pursuits in marriage

Even in the most hard conflict situations, you can address many commonplace easy factors which may be really based on our not unusual humanity. The elegant point is that every people may be understood and want to discover an answer. Everyone may locate it hard to discover their right message. There is a famous susceptible factor in emotional strain and stress, despite the fact that this may be tested in some other manner. Despite the anxiety that would arise in a warfare, there can be normally one common difficulty: do not attempt to damage anybody.

Tips for growing a not unusual interest in marriage

Listen and recognize every other element of view: you could additionally thank a person for paying attention to you. Remember that even while you're amazing, information is an essential area to begin. Customize the speak with the aid of manner of expression whilst the dialogue is not smooth and also you want the communicate to go properly notwithstanding the pressure. Pay hobby and apprehend the steps of the discussionsmall and massive. Refer to regions of settlement even as discussing one-of-a-kind issues.

Define commonplace desires. When you switch your hobby to the problems mentioned, it is frequently clean to find out that there are commonplace goals, no matter the versions in how they may be carried out.

Lessons of famous hobby in marriage

The prospect of not unusual pursuits encourages us to move past the choice to "display our thing of view", "be right" or every different intense decide. Common floor enables to apprehend and take transport of a complex state of affairs. It allows us to recognition on our behavior, as well as at the behavior of others.

If you don't forget commonplace floor, this can be a beneficial manual to get once more on it if the negotiations are at a vain prevent. Also, a common hobby is a foundation that wants to be elevated in order that the areas of the settlement turn out to be larger and large.

People tend to react the identical manner to situations until the pattern is broken. It is sufficient for someone to begin highlighting commonplace floor, so his negotiating companion may be greater willing to do the equal. You despite the fact that don't agree, the whole lot is in orderthe key's that a not unusual language presents an antidote to the models that contribute to warfare and create distance.

Common pursuits consequences disappear from sight in struggle situations. Situations emerge as exaggerated at the same time as every body tries to steer or weaken. It isn't unexpected that human beings neglect about areas of mutual interest, lose the capability to understand, examine and rely upon what they already have in common.

Chapter 17: Creating Moments Of Sharing: Daily Activities, Couple Rituals, Future Projects, Smiling And Having Fun Together

Everyone brings a semblance of formality and way of existence right right into a dating. The trouble is, there's in no manner any room for two, and seldom are people raised from the equal situation and state of affairs. You might have been married earlier than and function powerful ritual techniques you have a laugh anniversaries or vacations. Your associate could in all likelihood have grown up as an only toddler and isn't used to sharing location. Coming from exquisite worlds can reason friction, or it could be regarded as a terrific place to begin for a trendy life.

The Blending of Two Worlds

A important courting that leads to marriage will advise blending all your character family rituals, traditions, beliefs, and values. It's regularly much less complicated to allow numerous them bypass and truly start from scratch. The reasons you carefully keep in mind the values and beliefs of the alternative individual at the same time as embarking on a dating route end up painfully clean at this thing. When base-line values, goals, and ideals are too off, the connection will war. It's normally referred to as being inconsistently yoked and may spell disaster for the future plans of the relationship.

It doesn't imply that the mountains are impassable. All you want to do is search for the proper valleys and paths to make your manner over, spherical, and through them. Every vital dating has had to cope with those problems, but many didn't supply it an awful lot idea earlier. It's difficult to look the possible warning signs and symptoms and symptoms of future battle whilst the whole lot appears to be amusing, new, and exciting. Eventually, the truth of the scenario sets in and also you study that forming your rituals and traditions is typically the less tough direction.

The Importance of Rituals and Traditions

Rituals and traditions rule your existence greater than you may think about within the meanwhile. It quantities to almost each repeated motion we take, whether or now not it's excursion instances, precise days, or an ordinary meal. Let explore what a number of those are, so you can have a higher photograph of what you could have to deal with whilst blending lives.

What are Rituals?

Rituals are actions you are taking frequently, usually on a every day or weekly basis. Some of those are lifelong and difficult to break. A few examples of rituals are:

• Sitting down on the desk for meals or ingesting within the the front of the television.

• Daily exercise normal.

• Jogging or on foot each day.

• Certain days for chores like laundry or vacuuming.

What are Traditions?

Traditions are belongings you do, locations you cross, and uniqueness gadgets you devour or drink for unique sports. Holidays are typically full of traditions.

A few examples are:

• New Year's Eve and Champagne.

• Birthday dinner out.

• Thanksgiving meal prep at home or with own family.

• Valentine's Day expectations.

• Christmas gift putting in.

All individual rituals and traditions will ought to be explored to appearance when you have a few common ground. Many instances, the traditions and rituals want to get replaced for ones that artwork wonderful for each of you.

Holidays, Birthdays and Anniversaries

Unless you're a couple that doesn't care to have a laugh any holidays, anniversaries, or birthdays, you could must perform a little artwork to try to combo the traditions which is probably favorable to each of you. Each will consist of their very non-public memories and family traditions and the consequences can be a few component new that is each a hybrid of every or a very new advent.

Blending traditions

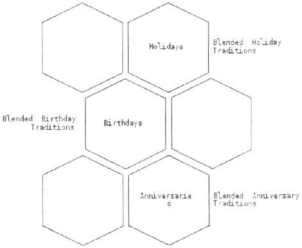

One instance of mixing traditions is even as you experience cooking a pleasing birthday meal, but your companion can not cook dinner dinner. You can continuously mixture the traditions. You prepare dinner their birthday meal and they take you out to a restaurant for yours. It's the right combination and answer.

Creating Memories and Standards

The vital a part of coming together as a couple is to speak about what is exciting to you approximately outstanding rituals and traditions. No rely how you make a decision to continue as a pair, make high-quality memories and set the necessities you want on your personal new own family. You can genuinely veer from all of the rituals and traditions you already know and set up new ones.

Create More than You Borrow

A a laugh and interesting part of turning into a sturdy couple is to establish new traditions and rituals which is probably specially your personal. Borrowing the components which is probably an essential a part of your beyond and incorporating them can be finished, however make sure you communicate the whole thing to the issue of being comfortable with any picks. Create new rituals and traditions based totally completely at the assets you like to do and are essential as a couple. Where will your new combined pursuits take you? Maybe you will start taking summer time holidays and make that a way of life. Perhaps it will probably be sitting at a fave café on the weekends eating a latte. It's all as loads as you and your partner.

Appreciate the New Traditions and Rituals

Enjoy and apprehend all the new traditions and rituals, further to any blended ones you design to your joint lives. Your existence collectively will maintain to conform, and the each day verbal exchange practiced will help you change topics up as you observe in form. You would in all likelihood need to hold with some rituals and traditions for your private. It's pleasant as long as you make bigger a healthful quantity of ones you may revel in together.

Chapter 18: Learn To Communicate And Listen To Each Other All The Time: Not Only Love But Complicity

I desire the two of you bring up "I" statements, non-verbal communique, and dialectical conduct remedy. As , this direction of therapy in psychology has numerous attributes, however the vital one is the concept of confronting one hassle at a time in choice to being overwhelmed with the useful useful resource of all of the capacity issues that might arise. With those 3 communique capabilities under your belt, you will be nicely-prepared for dealing with any troubles in communication that could come your manner.

I need to function every other conversation capability that you must upload to your listing of capabilities in verbal exchange which you need to take a look at, and that is lively listening.

You can get plenty extra out of conversation together with your partner even as you're an active listener. It way you don't truly lead them to accept as genuine with you're listening so they'll be aware of you higher, but you surely do be privy to them.

This in truth advantages you ultimately, as it enables you advantage valuable statistics. It tells you what is on their mind, that might pleasant permit you to your courting. Maybe you don't commonly make as a terrific deal attempt as you need to to get into your huge different's mind, but it is really clearly really worth the small problem.

You are positive to have determined examples of effective conversation between couples on your every day existence. Discuss wholesome, aware couples you understand and find struggle choice strategies that you every like.

Before, you probably did a similar interest, but it come to be within the context of what makes a wedding artwork. This time, I need your recognition to be on only the function of conversation in a conscious married dating.

Not most effective that, but I want you to invite yourselves what precise verbal exchange competencies you found could be the most useful to you for your precise troubles.

For instance, if one or each of you are constantly announcing you aren't listened to, each of you want to placed some strive into honing your lively listening. I say both of you need to do it due to the reality this is how any self-improvement you're making in dialectical conduct remedy should be. You may additionally moreover have an concept of who is frequently chargeable for your head, however each of you need to do it besides.

For one element, at the same time as every spouses do the equal self-improvement practices, we steer clean of the problem of blame that we're constantly trying to avoid in this shape of remedy. For another, you will but get fee out of it even if you don't assume you need it. People who're higher at lively listening than your common individual can nevertheless enhance; folks that can manipulate the tone in their voice very well can however discover ways to do it higher.

This is an vital issue to do due to the truth at the same time as this workbook can provide you with system to tackle any scenario on your marriage, making use of these device in your actual existence may be more realistic if you may see them in motion.

So a long way, you've got got gotten mainly deep into verbal exchange subjects, and you've got finished a number of the physical activities within the workbook, but most of your publicity to communique skills were absolutely theoretical. Now, you have to take the threat to repair that with the beneficial resource of doing practice for each of the conversation skills we've got were given included.

For energetic listening, you and your partner can listen to the radio or podcasts together. The capture is, one in every of you ought to quiz the possibility on little pieces of information they heard in the software program application to make sure they may be absolutely listening.

To workout controlling the emotional expression we make as a part of nonverbal communique. We can look in a mirror with wonderful facial expressions, imagining the emotions that go with them. Next, we're able to get the ones equal feelings into our imaginations, however without displaying them on our faces.

This effective expertise is called country manage, and it's far particularly useful to prevent humans from getting disenchanted with the emotions they take a look at on our faces.

State control isn't always taught almost enough as a communique device in remedy for couples, however it's miles an critical trouble of dialectical behavioral remedy. The cause for this is a clean false impression. People assume it's miles a way of washing all our feelings away and providing a clean slate, but this isn't the case in any respect.

The more correct manner to understand kingdom control is to appearance once more at the times while you have been a toddler. Back then, you didn't recognize any degree of united states of america of the united states control. No one did at that age. When you didn't get your manner, you cried until you probably did. When you felt like crying or screaming, you virtually did it. You didn't permit each person save you you.

Everyone stops this infantile lack of emotional manage once they start adulthood at least, this indicates that everyone has some diploma of state manipulate. The satisfactory distinction is how a whole lot nation manipulate they've got. There are a stunning type of individuals who can't seem to govern any of the non-verbal indicators that inform others what emotions they're feeling.

We may additionally all should look at a notable baseline of united states manipulate as a manner to live in society, however that doesn't propose we're all in addition appropriate at it. Some human beings can't seem to control themselves even into adulthood, and others appear as despite the fact that they aren't affected by feelings the least bit.

All nation manipulate comes all the way all the way down to enhancing the manage of the emotions you have got already were given. Whether you've got got lots or very little control of your emotions, you could make your emotions end up plenty much less and plenty less part of your out of doors presentation if you art work at it.

Remember that nation manipulate doesn't propose no longer feeling the way you enjoy. It manner now not displaying all of it to honestly anyone. You already understand the manner to do that particularly from growing up; all you want to do is get even higher at it.

All of the communication abilties included to this point can be practiced and reviewed. You and your partner can workout them collectively to reveal every other you're important about running through your fights.

Chapter 19: Intimacy And Sex: Opening Up Without Shame And Keeping Desire Alive

Now it's time to take it to a today's degree and to decorate elements of your sex life as well. This is specially crucial for those who've been in a dating with the equal person for a while. Things may moreover additionally start to enjoy a chunk silly and intercourse drives won't be as robust as they end up. This is the right time to begin rebuilding that sexual relationship collectively along with your accomplice thru attempting new subjects, speakme approximately personal desires, and gambling a laugh games. We may be exploring the subsequent subjects; growing couple intimacy, spicing up your sex life, trying new positions, playing new video video games and communicating your sexual needs/desires.

Increase Couple Intimacy

As your courting progresses, it's miles crucial to keep intercourse and lust alive, at the identical time as you turn out to be frequently increasingly comfortable with someone, it is able to put off a number of the mystery, that is because there's now not the satisfaction of studying someone and having the whole lot you do together be current day. At the begin of a dating, you are so keen to have sex with every exclusive due to the reality the other character is new and heat and a novelty of sorts. As you get used to them, it is able to be smooth to lose those feelings and settle into the comfortability of everything (like their frame or your habitual). This is never a horrible difficulty. Getting to date on your courting is a laugh and comforting in its manner, and isn't just like, however in a few strategies higher than, the early degrees. From a sexual perspective, regardless of the fact that, we don't want the approaching of this degree of your dating to deliver with it the surrender of interesting intercourse lifestyles.

If you are an prolonged-time period or married couple, you have got probable attempted every one of the traditional sex positions collectively from missionary to 69. You have probably furthermore evolved a habitual of your preferred positions and the order in that you do them through now. While you possibly apprehend the manner to please each unique locate it irresistible's 2d nature, rediscovering each particular's our our bodies in a sexy way and gaining know-how of latest techniques to pleasure every unique is right for couples who have been together for a long time.

At the start of a courting, you may have started out having sex casually in advance than you obtain collectively romantically, or you can have commenced having sex while you have grow to be a pair. Either manner, the start of any dating comes with an entire lot of uncharted territories. You are exploring a brand new character's complete body-internal and out, and letting them see all of yours. Of path, this may be nerve-wracking. There is probably some positions and sexual sports activities which you acquired't be without a doubt cushty doing with this person but, even if you have accomplished them in advance than with a person else. There are certain positions you may stay with which may be extra cushty on the begin of a courting, and that is excellent for studying a person's body and what they decide on. These positions serve us well while we're newly having sex with someone and are searching out the notable manner to help each other orgasm. You may think which you are well beyond this diploma in an extended-term dating. This degree of discovery, however, is a few aspect that we need to go again to once in a while. This is because of the truth we want to rediscover the person's frame and what they pick out as though it's miles the primary time we are exploring it. People's desires alternate and their our our bodies exchange. It is vital to continue to recognize a way to pleasure your companion as they broaden and alternate, and to expect the identical from them for your self. Further, revisiting our accomplice's frame with an open mind as though we apprehend not anything about it may be a amusing and flirty manner to renew zest on your intercourse life.

Importance of Spicing Up Your Sex Life

The most crucial importance of spicing up your sex life is to increase intimacy among you and your accomplice. Not simplest does this help your sex existence come to be greater fun and thrilling, but it moreover improves the communication and bond between you and your associate. We may be studying intimacy and the location that it plays in romantic relationships. We are going to study how you may paintings to preserve intimacy collectively along with your companion and what wearing out a greater stage of intimacy can and could do in your dating.

Intimacy can be very important among people while part of a couple, specifically inside the mattress room. Intimacy is what brings you shut and keeps you close up. Firstly, we are capable of check what intimacy manner and the only of a type varieties of intimacy that exist. There are extraordinary types of intimacy, and right right here I will define them for you earlier than digging deeper into the intimacy that exists among couples. Intimacy, in a wellknown revel in, is defined as mutual openness and vulnerability amongst two people. There are terrific methods in which you can offer and acquire openness and vulnerability in a dating. Intimacy does not need to encompass a sexual dating (despite the fact that it can). Therefore, it isn't excellent reserved for romantic relationships. Intimacy can also be observed in special types of near relationships like friendships or own family relationships. Below, I will define the perfect styles of intimacy.

Emotional Intimacy

Emotional intimacy is the capability to explicit oneself maturely and overtly, fundamental to a deep emotional connection among human beings. Saying things like "I love you" or "you're very crucial to me" are examples of this. It is likewise the capacity to respond in a mature and open manner while a person expresses themselves to you thru pronouncing such things as "I'm sorry" or "I love you too." This shape of open and inclined talk consequences in an emotional connection. For a deep emotional connection to shape, there should be a mutual willingness to be prone and open with one's deeper mind and emotions. This is in which this form of emotional intimacy comes from.

Intellectual Intimacy

Intellectual intimacy is a form of intimacy that includes discussing and sharing mind and opinions on highbrow topics, from which they advantage achievement and feelings of closeness with the opportunity individual. For example, if you are discussing politics with someone who you deem to be an highbrow identical, you could locate that you feel a closeness with them as you proportion your thoughts and reviews and be part of on an intellectual level. Many people locate thoughts and brains to be sexy in a partner!

Shared Interests and Activities

This form of intimacy is much much less well-known, however it is also considered a form of intimacy. When you proportion sports with a few one-of-a-kind character that you every experience and are obsessed on, this creates a experience of connection. For example, while you prepare dinner together or excursion collectively. These shared testimonies provide you with recollections to percent and this effects in bonding and intimacy (openness and vulnerability). This form of connection is commonly found in friendships, in familial relationships, and further importantly, in romantic relationships. Being able to share hobbies and sports consequences in a closeness that can be defined as intimacy.

Physical Intimacy

Physical intimacy is the sort that most people endure in mind after they pay interest the time period "intimacy," and it's far the kind that we're capable of be maximum concerned with interior this workbook, as it's far the shape of intimacy that consists of intercourse and all sports activities associated with sex. It moreover entails excellent non-sexual kinds of bodily touch which incorporates hugging and kissing. Physical intimacy can be determined in close to friendships or familial relationships wherein hugging and kisses on the cheek are common, but it is most often determined in romantic relationships.

Physical intimacy is the form of intimacy concerned whilst people are trying to make every specific orgasm. Physical intimacy is form of generally required for orgasm. Physical intimacy doesn't always imply that you are in love with the individual you're having intercourse with; it truely method that you are doing some issue intimate with each one of a kind person physical.

It is likewise possible to be intimate with your self, and at the same time as this starts offevolved with the emotional intimacy of self-attention, it moreover includes the physical intimacy of masturbation and bodily self-exploration. I define sexual, the physical intimacy of the self as being in touch with the components of your self physical that you can not normally be in touch with. If you're a woman, your breasts, your clitoris, your vagina, and your anus. If you're a man, your testicles, your penis, your anus. Being able to be bodily intimate with yourself permits you to have greater exciting sex, greater pleasant orgasms, and a extra terrific general dating collectively with your body. Allowing a person to be bodily intimate with you in a sexual manner is likewise an emotionally intimate revel in, irrespective of your dating with the character. Being in price of your very very own body even as it's far within the palms of a few special person may be very essential and that is why masturbation is that this form of key detail to bodily intimacy.

You can bear in mind bodily intimacy as some aspect that breaks the barrier of personal place. By this definition, this consists of touching of any kind, but particularly sexual intercourse, kissing touching, and some detail else of a sexual nature. When you're having intercourse with anyone, regardless of whether or not or no longer you have got were given romantic feelings for them or not, you're having a bodily intimate courting with them. The difference amongst a courting that consists of bodily intimacy alone and no unique forms of intimacy and a romantic relationship is that a romantic relationship will even contain emotional intimacy, shared sports activities and intellectual intimacy is that a deep and lasting romantic courting will want to embody all of these types of intimacy proper away.

New Positions to Try

When it entails intercourse, changing the positions you operate is the critical component to preserving it thrilling and unique. After a short time, a sexual ordinary can emerge as silly and antique, because of the truth what to anticipate at every turn and what to do subsequent without questioning in any respect. Your mind, coronary coronary heart, and frame do no longer need to be engaged like they're at the same time as you are doing some issue new and thrilling that is turning you on. When you're appearing a intercourse role that you have in no manner attempted earlier than, your complete frame is engaged, thinking about what's next, feeling new sensations, seeking to the other individual to look if they're feeling pleasure as well. This can be very one-of-a-type from acting a characteristic you've got have been given achieved frequently over. This is why converting your sex positions is beneficial; it engages every a part of you. I might be coaching you approximately some new positions that you and your accomplice can try to spice topics up a piece!

Chapter 20: Children: How To Become Parents Together

Parenting is a hobby-changer to all marriages. In many methods, it is able to trade the connection dynamic for the better or worse, relying on the ideal set of instances. In television commercials supplying infant bathe playing cards, diapers, and a litany of toddler merchandise, parenting, and marriage are depicted as natural bliss and handy. Your family will promote you a tale about how toddlers are a heaven-sent package deal deal of happiness – and they may be – however they pass the hard work that is going into making it all art work!

Of course, it is critical to like our youngsters. But it is crucial to be alive to what parenting does to marriages. There isn't always any reason that loving your toddler and working on your marriage want to be collectively excellent. A glad marriage almost constantly way a satisfied toddler. Marriage happiness, sustainability, and truly certainly well worth are preferred at the hip with parenting.

Studies into the relationship among marriage and parenting mean that most relationships exchange for the more severe whilst couples transition into households. Initially, annoying for the child way sleepless nights, a surge in needs in bringing up the little one, and an abundance of latest expectations for every parents. The mother and father furthermore should keep down the necessities of a activity. Between 30 and 50 percentage of couples that become dad and mom face huge pressure and depression.

University of California, Berkeley researchers, establishes that more than 70 percentage of all new mothers confronted a marked decline of their marital delight. Around one-0.33 of recent dad and mom experience massive depression after turning into parenting. One-8th of all couples that transition into mother and father revel in divorce by the time their toddlers hit 18 months.

Shifting from enthusiasts to parents may be tumultuous in your marriage. The transition shakes the principles of your circle of relatives participants. The stop end result is large disruption of the everyday go with the drift of records among partners. It also upends the popularity quo of feelings and man or woman responsibilities. In short, there is a getting to know curve for the enthusiasts after they become parents. Completing the analyzing and adjusting because of this is important to the fulfillment of parenting and marriage.

The emotional disruption is especially pushed thru the adjustments within the normal social dynamics. For example, a walking mother's lifestyles shifts from the bubbly workplace colleagues for breastfeeding, handling mountains of laundry, and bottle-washing. After round six months, she faces the danger of converting again to her taking walks routine. The husband has to paintings with the spouse via the complete system. However, most fathers experience not noted of the early years of worrying for the kid. The traditional give up end result is each of the spouses is doing more, the communication lines and frequency declines, and each revel in massively underappreciated.

As the kid grows, you all at once discover yourself considering your little one may be enrolled within the right preschool utility. You fear whether or not your daughter or son is inside the proper track, paintings, and tumbling little infants' instructions.

Can Parenting be used to Strength Marriages?

It is not smooth. It is difficult. But marriage may be used to sweeten your marriage, make it stronger, and long-lasting! Most people view parenting as a set of stressors an amazing manner to make your existence depressing and probably boost up the save you of your courting along side your associate. However, with the right touch, parenting can be the glue that holds you collectively. In this regard, it'll advantage your relationship similarly to the well-being of the kid(s).

All you can do to leverage parenting in improving your courting inside a marriage is to put your courting first. Recognizing that your marriage is a bit in development is going an extended manner to cementing your determination in the direction of bolstering your bonds. Working for your versions usually additionally allows red meat up the guidelines of your courting on the equal time as ironing out disagreements earlier than they grow to be extra widespread issues.

A cognizance on appreciating each one of a type at the same time as minimizing grievance is crucial in sweetening your relationship. Communication is the underlying basis of a dating. Maintaining the bidirectional drift of statistics, opinions, views, and perspectives is critical, maintaining the passion to hold a dating of married spouses with a infant(s).

Using parenting as a tool to enhance your dating incredible and sustainability desires a planned effort focused on the dynamics of parenting. Understanding the predicted disruptions to the relationship parenting brings will assist you be better organized. It additionally technique that you are better geared up to harness the parenting changes and making them paintings to your dating.

Learning approximately parenting and getting equipped for the shifts it brings want to embody both spouses. This approach ought to be collaborative first of all because of the reality every of you may want the statistics and abilties to transport through the upcoming adjustments. Secondly, a concerted method is probably to obtain maintaining a running and powerful relationship. When each of you put inside the art work, you are vulnerable to shoulder the burden equitably. Although parenting cannot biologically be equitable, it creates a experience that the husband is supportive of the wife within the direction of this era.

The venture managing maximum couples going into marriage is that they'll be now not organized for the disruptions of parenting.

They aren't geared up for the upending in their lives they face after the infant is born, and parenting starts offevolved. As a quit end result, parenting turns into overwhelming, bodily, and emotionally. This effects in a surge in conflicts and an growth inside the chance of divorce or unhappy marriages/relationships.

Here are some pointers on how you could use parenting as a platform to construct a stronger and prolonged-lasting courting and marriage:

Talk about the Certainties and Uncertainties Ahead

Talking approximately uncertainties does not make them any more assured. However, it's going to help you be emotionally organized and fantastic of yourself while navigating through the moments and situations of parenting.

It is also essential to plan and ventilate some of an appropriate issues, which incorporates splitting errands and household chores. It is critical to talk approximately in which the income of the circle of relatives will come from. In this situation, it's miles vital to answering the following questions: who is going to be the breadwinner? And who is going to live at home rearing the child?

Talk approximately the day-care opportunity. Establish who receives your toddler to the day-care middle and who receives him/her once more. Explore the trouble of a babysitter, the fee variety for this option, and plan your lives round what you agree. Figure out how night time time time shift duties can be break up, who is going to smooth or sterilize the breast pump and bottles each day. Figure out the shopping time table, cooking plan, and cleansing chores.

These statistics appear small and innocent. But without figuring out the department of difficult paintings regarding those factors, they could make contributions to frustration, strain, and despair. If left unsorted, they could gnaw away at the connection.

However, figuring them out creates an know-how and collaborative approach that is healthful in your courting. It additionally establishes a revel in that everyone is doing their truthful percent. Moreover, developing a concise plan on managing the ones chores and responsibilities reduces the opportunities that you will be crushed as a pair at the same time as parenting begins. Emotionally, you'll be organized for the deluge of responsibilities and obligations, that permits you to make it markedly extra comfortable to deal with and transition into the parenting position.

Focus on the Downside of Parenthood with the View of Avoiding its Pitfalls on the Marriage

Maintaining a great and hopeful notion of parenting is crucial for present day fathers and moms. But it's miles critical to shield in competition to lofty expectancies as a way to be shattered by means of the truth of fatherhood and motherhood.

Yes, toddlers provide big delight, and they bring about lots of happiness to a wedding. They additionally bring an uptick in physical and emotional hard work that can take their toll on the connection. Bathing the child, feeding, thrilling, and changing the child 24 hours a day and 7 hours each week are stressful chores. All couples should be emotionally and physical organized for such wishes in advance than they begin their roles as dad and mom.

Focusing on and speakme approximately the downside(s) of parenting is vital in marriage. It will will permit you to deal with the changes and disruptions in your lives. It is good enough to talk about your fatigue, frustrations, or maybe anger together with your accomplice. Ensure, to be honest collectively with your associate regarding those issues and additionally keeping a supportive stance.

Feeling anger, frustration, and fatigue does not suggest which you are a horrible determine. It is important to confess the ones feelings and popularity on working together to treatment them within the marriage. This method permits in disarming the ones emotions and as a end result prevents them from negatively affecting your courting.

For instance, you could agree earlier that if one in every of you is beaten and isn't always able to fulfill their chores, the opposite will cover and cope with the toddler for some time. This gives an possibility of comfort for the overwhelmed partner. It moreover establishes a collectively supportive dynamic that deepens your affection for each unique within the midst of a difficult length.

Fatigue, frustrations, or perhaps anger because of anger can marinate into greater brilliant problems within the marriage. For instance, those feelings can with out trouble bring about resentment of each specific, lack of believe, and a conversation breakdown. By that specialize in everyday and sincere verbal exchange, you will typically apprehend how your associate is feeling constantly. You can render your assist once they need it and shoulder a number of their worry and uncertainty.

Maintain Honesty approximately Gains and Losses

In frequently, parenting will bring about some earnings and losses. For example, you have got acquired the child of your goals. He/she melts your coronary coronary coronary heart each time you spot them. However, you can't keep away from feeling sad and empty because of the shortage of your chosen sex lifestyles. For the mom, you misplaced your smooth pre-infant length 8s and replaced them with elastic-waist denims.

Most new parents typically complain, silently, approximately the disruption to their lives occasioned thru the usage of the child and their parenting responsibilities and duties. These lawsuits and silent resentment purpose the marital distance to widen. In a few intense instances, it is able to bring about shame and a decline in arrogance.

For instance, a new daddy also can revel in changed with the aid of way of the toddler in his spouse's existence and affection. The mother might be aggravated and even sad about the processes parenting (being pregnant, nursing, and the rigors of childcare) have transformed her frame. These emotions are everyday amongst new mother and father.

Sharing such emotions of loss, shame, or disruption is important in dealing with the emotional toll of parenting. Maintaining honesty approximately the ones problems along with your accomplice helps you to experience higher and enhance your bond as a couple.

Communication concerning the ones emotions allows set up a angle for behavior. For example, emotions of loss might probably make the mother snappy and aggravated, which can in all likelihood spill over to her interactions with other people, in conjunction with the husband. The husband may show feelings and reactions which may be out of the norm.

Through conversation and honesty, you can kind via those feelings and offer an reason for the context of behavior. The resulting knowledge will create rigor room for a learning curve and a few region for the increase and improvement of your dating.

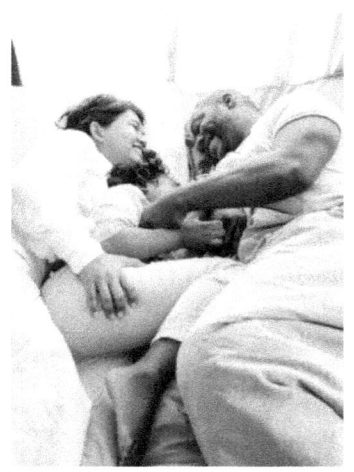

Chapter 21: Work And Finances: Respect Each Other's Work Needs And Find A Fair Compromise, Deciding Together How To Invest Your Money

When a man and a girl are residing as a couple, or when they have a marriage undertaking, it is uncommon to pay attention them talk the difficulty of economic manage. However, in keeping with several studies, the economic query is at the beginning of numerous divorces. Being in a relationship is not quite plenty love. It's wonderful to love each exceptional, but it does now not pay for buying, cinema, or travelling in Beijing. So how do you control your coins in a courting? Of path, as there's no character way to be in love, there may be no miracle recipe for coping with one's budget with one's life associate. That can be why we every now and then see amazing relationships that lead to violent conflict because of money. Thus, to keep away from those cash manage issues that are a real wasp nest to your marriage, here are some pointers.

Set priorities

In the life of a pair, it's far perfectly reasonably-priced and understandable that everybody can have unique behavior and desires than the opportunity. And it's far regular to try and answer them reasonably, with out penalizing one or the alternative. Only, it need to be stated that existence as a couple calls for a certain big style of picks, even sacrifices. It's therefore crucial to apprehend the manner to make options whilst thinking about the choice of every one among a kind.

Also, it is crucial, and principally, to define the way of running together, to set up a price range, even earlier, and to do not forget monetary financial savings and investments. It is regular for couples to divide their each day obligations to make their lives less complicated. However, as regards to your monetary technique, it's critical to talk approximately it and pick a line to observe. You in all likelihood have joint projects that require man or woman and collective sacrifices on which you may ought to agree. Listening is the great manner to getting alongside.

The 3 healthful ways of spending in a dating: The financial control of the couple is a spectrum that is built spherical 3 strategies: fairness, half of and a half of of, and pooling. There is a tremendous concept at the same time as every of you compromise. Fairness way that everybody participates in step with their income. Sometimes one associate earns considerably extra than the other or has precise goals; it can, therefore, make a contribution greater than the latter without this being unfair. Half and a 1/2 of is the method so that you can succeed while each individuals of the couple have the equal monetary person (debt, leisure, income). They will percent the prices. Pooling is acting without regard to who can pay what. The couple serves as a unmarried entity in income and prices.

Communicating together together with your spouse

Even if one involves a selection to have separate money owed and price range, it is critical to talk with one's associate about the whole lot related to investments (loans and amazing debts). And that is all of the greater important while you consider that a elegant account has been created. You ought to not have monetary secrets and techniques. Having thriller money owed may be the deliver of unsightly surprises. Moreover, if one of the companions disappeared or is deceased. An obnoxious assumption but no matter the fact that possible, being privy to the critiques and bills of the deceased simplifies the existence of the survivor.

Create a not unusual account

To placed into exercise the 3 healthy approaches of monetary manipulate, couples will ought to select out how they may manage their coins in a economic institution. This comes down to 3 alternatives too: joint account, a separate account, or each.

Separate bills permit seeing the charges and contribution of each. Each accomplice can, consequently, bear his percent of duty and the stableness is rapid located. However, this solution may additionally once in a while no longer be only. A couple is likewise a -person journey that consists of a whole lot of shared fees. Tracking can grow to be complicated. The joint account makes it lots much less complicated to hold tune of the couple's expenses. For those who preference to pool their coins, this can be an high-quality solution. That said, the joint account requires greater manipulate and session to keep away from ugly surprises. But, on the same time as preserving a sure autonomy and a personal financial area, it's far feasible to spend together for joint projects. This is the incredible of each structures but additionally concentrates on their faults. It might require greater logistics.

The creation of a good sized account makes it possible to simplify the participation of every one within the ordinary charges and the check-up of the expenses and the charge variety. Then you have to feed the account for the normal costs. Each associate has, of direction, the liberty to maintain a non-public account, which he can control independently via keeping a discretionary income. As for the control of this account, we need to try and allocate the price range to the not unusual priorities. We want to additionally try to be rigorous, however without depriving ourselves of everything. This might in all likelihood recommend that if one spouse dreams some factor that doesn't jeopardize the couple's rate range, the alternative spouse need to allow him or her to buy it.

Once you have got made the monetary alternatives, you may pass about your relationship without demanding greater than you need to about cash. In the give up, pinnacle money owed make accurate relationships.

Balancing the price range

Achieve and preserve a balanced finances via dividing normal charges based totally on each person's profits. As an instance, if one of the spouses earns 10,000 bucks at the same time as the other earns 5,000 dollars, the one who makes greater have to assume -thirds of the home costs, whilst the opportunity one should pay absolutely the last 0.33.

As brief due to the reality the situation of the couple evolves, it's miles important to modify and adapt to the budget. This is, as an instance, the case while the own family is growing or whilst buying a house. Moreover, now not living past one's technique is an awesome manner to accumulate a balanced budget, evoked actually above, to assemble precautionary monetary financial savings, and to order an funding functionality.

But we need to in any respect expenses restrict purchases on credit score rating rating and, especially, question its intake behavior. Small every day and recurring expenses can be pleasant sums for which you can find a higher use.

If one of the spouses is thrifty even as the alternative is a spender, try and discover the stability by way of way of defining the obligations of each. In extraordinary phrases, it's far critical to establish who does what. The perfect would be a superb supervisor who gives with the control of high fee range. But conversation need to stay, that the choice-making stays shared and that the opportunity can anticipate exclusive responsibilities in the couple.

Also, even in case you do now not have investment duties, a monetary representative can be of exceptional help to you. You can start together together with your banker, as an example. To be satisfied together collectively together with your simplest banker is however no longer simply apt. The super factor in finance stays to research. You may be self sustaining and keep control of your investments.

Contrary to what you can keep in mind, it isn't so complicated. And many web sites and blogs are very well carried out and provide terrific recommendation. If no longer surely independent, education may even help you better apprehend the recommendation and tips of your monetary representative, ask applicable questions, and be surer of your

selections.

Money may be a supply of trouble and discord on your marriage. Take the lead, and those suggestions need to help you.

One very last tip: do now not hesitate to address the problem, even if you fear being taken for a person involved. In any case, the query of cash will come sooner or later. So skip! Moreover, through explaining your method, doubts may be lifted. And then you will pass for someone responsible and proactive.

Chapter 22: How To Face And Solve Conflicts

I is probably coaching you the significance of struggle resolution and a manner to do it peacefully. As all and sundry apprehend, each dating will come across battle and its very non-public set of arguments. How you approach to battle is especially important as it can make or smash your dating. We is probably that specialize in all subjects related to war decision; the importance of them, dealing with solvable dating problems, violent communique, and nonviolent communication, analyzing to apply nonviolent communication throughout conflicts, and restoring receive as genuine with after war. Remember, conflicts are normal inside relationships and the motive isn't to avoid any conflict viable. The factor is to genuinely be for the reason that conflicts do take place but to discover ways to navigate thru them so that you and your companion can discover a method to make more potent the relationship.

Conflict Resolution Skills Are Important

Since battle and arguments are an unavoidable part of life, it is essential to discover ways to speak yourself at some point of conditions like that. While it is able to seem like there are masses of factors to consider, it's going to come greater glaringly the greater you workout it. This will awareness on offering you with strategies and examples on a way to particular yourself during arguments and conflicts. Making judgments, blaming, yelling, shaming, and so on are sorts of conversation styles which you don't want to apply at some point of conflicts. As lengthy as you hold in thoughts those elements, you'll be able to specific your self in a nonviolent manner and the steps will come once more to your memory. Even in case you aren't following the steps too carefully, so long as you are ensuring that you are not the usage of violent verbal exchange, you will be lots towards the usage of nonviolent verbal exchange than in case you had forgotten everything you decided out absolutely.

Violent Communication Vs. Nonviolent Communication

We will study the difference among violent and nonviolent communication so that you have an concept of the way to tell them aside. Now which you understand what verbal exchange is on a fundamental degree, we're capable of dive a hint bit deeper and take a look at the difference among those strategies of verbal exchange. There is a completely skinny line amongst violent and non-violent communication, in order for someone to learn how to speak non-violently, they need to have the capacity to distinguish the two. Let's dive right in.

Oftentimes at the identical time as speaking, in particular in instances of battle, human beings will use approach of verbal exchange that can be taken into consideration "violent." While this does not mean bodily violence, we can be violent within the way that we talk. What this shows is speaking in a manner that effects in damage to a person else or ourselves. Violent verbal exchange is a way of conversation that consists of any wide sort of the subsequent;

- Judging

- Shaming

- Criticizing

- Ridiculing

- Demanding

- Coercing

- Labeling

- Threatening

- Blaming

- Accusing

When any or all the following are present in our communications, we are using violent conversation. Communicating on this way has terrible impacts on the humans with whom we're talking. As this is violent communication, it motives internal damage. If we're speaking intrapersonally on this manner, we may cause harm to ourselves. If we talk in this manner with others, we're capable of cause internal harm to others. In time, this form of verbal exchange can purpose anger and resentment, and if we speak to ourselves on this manner, it may finally result in despair.

Oftentimes, we don't even recognise we're using violent verbal exchange, as it may be pretty a ordinary way of interacting for us. Many societies model violent conversation and because of this, the individuals who extend up in them don't apprehend that there is another manner to speak. This reasons many interactions to be whole of anger and hate and incorporate raised voices and cruel phrases. Sometimes, this results in physical violence.

Violent conversation goals to decrease someone's feelings of self-worth, ignores their desires, and is void of compassion. It can arise on each the part of the speaker and the listener. Below are some examples of various sorts of violent verbal exchange for your reference.

1. Moral Judgement or Evaluation

"Jennifer is lazy."

In this case, the speaker is the use of judgment. They are also labeling Jennifer and being crucial of her. They are comparing her and doing so in a judgmental manner. In this form of violent communication, the speaker frequently sees the opportunity individual as being wrong.

2. Denying Responsibility

"It's no longer my fault; the coverage states that I should fireplace you."

In this case of violent verbal exchange, the speaker is refusing to take obligation for his or her moves and blaming them on policies, policies, and policies. In this sort of example, the person might also moreover additionally blame their mind or feelings on exclusive people or guidelines, social tips, or whatever apart from their desire-making.

3.Demanding

"You want to do my homework for me."

In this type of instance, the speaker is implying (or from time to time explicitly mentioning) that there's the threat of punishment, of getting to take the blame, or of losing a reward inside the occasion that they do now not have a look at the decision for. This kind additionally can be seen within the reverse, in which there is the implication of a praise if the man or woman complies with the decision for. This is a manipulative shape of communique which is also a kind of name for.

4.Lack of Compassion

The Difference Between Violent and Nonviolent Communication

As you currently have seen each shape of conversation on their very personal, we're going to examine them. Violent communication has an inclination to be the kind that we turn to robotically and is the only that is modeled for us while we input the arena as youngsters. On the television, on public transit, or even in our houses growing up, we're uncovered to violent communication. A person isn't always frequently capable of conduct themselves using high-quality nonviolent verbal exchange in a global that solutions them with violent communication, but it's far feasible.

Violent conversation strategies interactions using negative assumptions and judgments towards unique people, and the whole lot this is stated comes from the ones assumptions. When one individual techniques an interaction in this way, the opportunity person or people typically have a tendency to get protective and they'll then moreover use violent communication. The quit end result is harm feelings, feelings of inadequacy, feeling judged and shamed, amongst others. These people who left this interplay feeling the ones strategies then approach their next interplay using violent verbal exchange due to the fact they're despite the fact that feeling harm by using way of manner of their very last interplay. The cycle then continues due to the fact the harm emotions and anger are exceeded from one person to the subsequent over and over once more.

On the other, whilst a person processes an interplay from an area of emotional vulnerability and being open to discovering the opportunity human beings within the interaction in region of judging them, the possibility people will normally normally have a tendency to reply thru additionally showing emotional vulnerability and real task for the nicely-being of others. When this is exceeded on from interplay to interaction in region of violent verbal exchange and anger, humans leave with amazing emotions in place of terrible ones.

Changing the interactions that you have with human beings is not smooth, specifically in case you experience judged or shamed via manner of using the phrases of others. It takes one individual in the interplay to be courageous sufficient to technique it in a loving and actual manner to turn it round, and that is how NVC can spread.

In an extended-term relationship including that among spouses or companions, the form of verbal exchange you use will have a notable effect at the health and durability of your relationship. Not best in times of battle but in everyday interactions along with your partner, the manner which you method their feelings and their dreams creates pretty an impact within the long term. It has been demonstrated that the durability of a marriage is essentially depending on the potential of the partners to understand the dreams of the alternative and help them in meeting the ones dreams. This ties into nonviolent communication as it focuses carefully at the needs of human beings and the emotions that are associated with them. By the use of compassion and a proper interest in assisting your associate improve their properly-being, you could have a wholesome and thriving courting.

The unique part of that is how your courting impacts your children. The first dating this is modeled for a child is the relationship among their mother and father. By the usage of nonviolent communique with every different, you are modeling a wholesome and respectful, deep and loving relationship. This concept of approaches a dating appears is a few trouble that your little one will take with them for the rest of their lifestyles and could form their expectations and thoughts of strategies they will conduct themselves of their relationship ultimately. It is important to recollect of this if you have children.

Learning Nonviolent Communication During Conflicts

Nonviolent communication can be used to treatment many styles of conflicts. These troubles can be things like finding out who takes your dog for a stroll or telling your baby to do their homework. While those do no longer need to be conflicts, every so often, via using violent conversation, they could change into them. By using nonviolent communique, you could stop this in advance than it happens. For instance:

If you and your associate are identifying who's going to take your dog for a walk:

"The dog desires to go out for a walk earlier than mattress. Having to walk him earlier than bed makes me experience demanding because of the fact I have to wake up early inside the morning and I want sleep. Would you be willing to take him for his before-bed walk?"

Or:

If you are telling your infant to do their homework: